To My Daughters

With Ballet in My Soul

Adventures of a Globetrotting Impresario

A Memoir by Eva Maze

⬤ Moonstone Press LLC . Sarasota, FL

Published in the United States

Moonstone Press LLC
4816 Carrington Circle, Sarasota, FL 34243

Executive Editor: Stephanie Maze
Senior Editor: Karin Kinney
Art Director: Alexandra Littlehales

Library of Congress Cataloging-in-Publication Data

Names: Maze, Eva, author.
Title: With ballet in my soul : adventures of a globetrotting impresario : a
    memoir / by Eva Maze.
Description: Sarasota, FL : Moonstone Press LLC, [2017]
Identifiers: LCCN 2016039275 | ISBN 9780983498384 (hardcover) | ISBN
    9780983498391 (eISBN)
Subjects: LCSH: Maze, Eva. | Dancers--United States--Biography. |
    Dancers--England--Biography. | Dancers--Russia (Federation)--Biography. |
    Women theatrical producers and directors--Biography. | Theatrical
    producers and directors--Biography
Classification: LCC GV1785.M367 A3 2017 | DDC 792.8092 [B] --dc23
LC record available at https://lccn.loc.gov/2016039275

Printed in Malaysia

Acknowledgments

I wish to thank the following people for their very valuable contributions to this memoir: my daughter, Stephanie, for overseeing the entire project, and patiently delving into 90 years of photographs, brochures, programs, and articles; Elinor Rogosin, adjunct instructor of writing at Sarasota's Ringling College of Art and Design and author of "Chasing Love" and "The Dance Makers," for transcribing the initial interviews with me and giving the book an early structure; and my good friend and former educator, Dr. Jean Mitchell, for all of her creative insights and suggestions. I also wish to thank text editor, Karin Kinney, and layout designer, Alexandra Littlehales, for their most welcomed expertise and commitment to this endeavor.

Table of Contents

Life is either a daring adventure or nothing.

— Helen Keller

1. Bucharest

My dreams of becoming a ballerina were shattered when I was diagnosed with scarlet fever in the Spring of 1929. "I can't see, Mamma. Mamma, I'm blind," I kept repeating over and over again. My body shook, racked with a very high fever, and I couldn't stop crying. "It will be fine," my mother whispered as she held me in her arms." The doctor is coming." My mother's voice was calm as she tried to soothe me, but nothing she said or did seemed to help. I was seven years old, exhausted, and terrified. In my panic, I remember a doctor coming to our house to deliver the verdict.

It was not unusual in those days for a child my age to come down with scarlet fever, or what was also known as "brain fever." Usually contracted at school, it would begin with a sore throat and rash, and once diagnosed, the entire family was isolated and quarantined. There were no vaccines or antibiotics then, and the child would often die.

Following a previous misdiagnosis – that of an ear infection – I was finally rushed to the hospital for an operation by a specialist, a 70-year-old ear, nose, and throat surgeon known as Professor Popovici. He ended up breaking the mastoid bones behind my ears to drain the

My mother, Liza, holding me,
August 1922

With my father, David,
after my operation, 1929

buildup of fluids from my brain. In today's world, this disease would have successfully been treated with antibiotics, but this was Bucharest, Romania, in 1929, and many medical advances lay in the future. The surgery was successful, and with two scars that, to this day, have remained behind my ears, I am indebted to Dr. Popovici for having saved my eyesight – and my life. While this was to be the most traumatic experience of my childhood, it taught me something perhaps more valuable that has carried me through life: to have courage.

As far back as I can remember, I had dreamt of becoming a ballerina, and though I eventually made a full recovery, my hopes of dancing on stage soon faded when my parents, concerned about my health, refused to allow me to exert myself physically in any way. Ballet classes I had previously taken and thoroughly enjoyed were now forbidden. I was their only child, and had almost died, so their overprotection was perhaps understandable, but I was very disappointed, especially since, prior to my illness, my mother had actually wanted me to study ballet. She had taken me to a ballet performance at the Opera House in Bucharest and, much to my delight, arranged for my first ballet lessons at the age of five. My teacher at the time – an imposing former Russian dancer named Madame Semeonova – thought I had a talent for ballet, and even offered me a scholarship. Once I had recovered completely, she did her best to convince my parents to have me resume my lessons, but they would have none of it. My mother had made up her mind that any strenuous activity, including ballet, would endanger my health.

I did, however, continue to dance around the house on my own, since moving my body to music came naturally to me. We all have different ways of expressing ourselves, and responding to beautiful music physically made me feel romantic and ethereal – as if I were floating on air. It would be another 13 years until I returned to my early love of ballet class when, as a young, married 20-year-old, I began training seriously in New York City. By then, I knew it was too late for me to have a professional career as a ballet dancer, though I continued to have a deep affection for the world of music and dance – and felt an almost mystical connection to it. Little did I know this feeling would eventually lead me to another fascinating career in the performing arts: that of managing and touring other talented dancers and artists. Though I myself would not end up dancing on stage in front of audiences around the world (other than in a few bit parts early in my professional life), I would do my best to work behind the scenes and instead, as what is known as an "impresario," bring the wonderfully artistic world of dance – and other highly creative theatrical mediums – directly to the myriads of passionate spectators who support them worldwide.

First things first, however…

To begin with, I was born in Bucharest, Romania, on a summer day in 1922. My father, David Feldstein, came from Kiev, the capital and most sophisticated city of the Ukraine, known for its imposing architecture and picturesque church domes. Originally part of Russia, Ukraine had attempted to gain independence from the Russians between 1918 and 1920. Failing to do so, it was subsequently absorbed into the Union of Soviet Socialist Republics as one of its original republics. This led to a flood of refugees from the Volga riverbanks into Ukraine, spreading typhus and cholera, and to a failure of crops that subsequently caused serious famine in the region. With chaos reigning throughout the republic, my father saw little hope for a promising future there, and chose to leave Kiev. Or perhaps "escape" might be a better word, for he decided to swim across the Dniester River at night, eluding Soviet border guards who were posted along the river's banks. My father, who was then in his late 20s, landed in Bessarabia – now known as Moldova – in the eastern region of Romania bordering Ukraine.

National borders had shifted dramatically across southeastern Europe after World War I,

My parents (left) as young newlyweds with friends in 1921

and regional borders fluctuated. Portions of the principality of Moldova had been annexed by the Russian Empire in 1912 by the treaty of Bucharest between the Ottoman Empire and Russia. Following the Russian Revolution in 1917, Moldova declared its independence from Russia and elected its own government. When World War I ended in 1918, Moldova – with a majority of its population speaking Romanian – decided to join Romania.

My father met my mother, Liza Feinsilber, in the small town of Soroca, Bessarabia, where she was born in 1888. One of six siblings, she had lived there her entire life, but soon moved to Bucharest, Romania, after falling in love with my father, and marrying him in 1920. I made my entrance into this world two years later.

Bucharest – often described as the "Paris of the Balkans" – was Romania's most sophisticated city in 1922, and offered the best opportunities for a comfortable lifestyle in the country. My parents spoke Russian at home – probably because my father preferred it to Romanian. Because of Russia's domination of Bessarabia and the fact that Russian was the first language taught in school, my mother spoke it as well. As a result, I was completely bilingual in Russian and Romanian at an

Class portrait with me smiling (2nd row), Institutul Sfantul Josef elementary school

early age. Though Jewish by birth, I attended a Catholic elementary school by the name of Institutul Sfantul Josef, and the nuns who ran the school taught us German and French. I was also tutored privately in English, and years later, when I started to earn a living, picked up two additional Romance languages: Spanish and Portuguese. I would eventually learn eight languages rather well (some more fluently than others). Looking back, I believe this early immersion in foreign languages is what motivated me to become interested the world outside of Romania, and develop a desire to expand my horizons. There was no television in those days, only radio, and I didn't see many movies, so it was these different languages that peaked my curiosity in other cultures. I've often been asked how I ended up as an international impresario: I can only say that this career choice originated out of a mixture of cultural experiences that began with my childhood in Romania.

Apart from my brief brush with death, my years in Bucharest were comfortable, and we lived a pleasant middle-class lifestyle. We were a close-knit family, and I particularly remember my favorite uncle Sioma – my mother's brother – treating me to lovely weekend rides through the wide, tree-lined boulevards of Bucharest, in a carriage drawn by white horses.

In my elementary school uniform, age 10

I was a good student in school, though somewhat lazy. Rather than pressure me to excel and win awards, my parents' only wish was for me to complete my assignments and pass each grade.

I was also a bit vain: The Catholic elementary school required us to attend school in black uniforms with white starched collars and cuffs, black stockings, and a blue velvet beret that was to be worn in a certain way. The nuns loved my mother, who always made sure that my school uniform was immaculate. I, however, would take every opportunity to alter my stiff uniform here and there, often coming to school with my beret slanted at an angle of my preference – which would promptly be rearranged by the nuns. I would also make a point to leave school in the afternoon wearing sheer black stockings (which were not allowed in this Catholic school), rather than the acceptable thicker tights – which I deemed ugly and would pull off in the bathroom at the end of the day. Perhaps these were early signs of my love of clothes and fashion – or perhaps, just a desire to be different.

My teenage education was spent at the Liceul Carmen Sylva, a Romanian lycée (middle and high school) named after a 19th-century writer and queen consort, Elizabeth I of Romania (Carmen Sylva was her pseudonym). I had my first romantic infatuation with a young man

Dancing at home in a Romanian costume

With high school friends (2nd from left)

17

With my parents' friends (first row, 2nd from right)   With my friends (top right)

named Titel (short for Aristide) Pappo. Titel was my first big love and at 16, a year older than I. He was handsome and very intelligent (he later became a doctor), and we were smitten with each other. Middle-class families in Bucharest usually kept housekeepers, and since Titel and I lived close to one another, our maids would act as go-betweens for both of us, often carrying love-letters back and forth by hand. Titel's letters were especially elegant: He had a way with words, and would always include quotes in Latin from Virgil or Cicero or another writer.

My family had a nice circle of friends, and teenagers would get together in their homes, at the movies or at the ice-skating rink, where the girls were chaperoned by their mothers. Romanians in general love to entertain and are known to be very hospitable. In those days, it was no different. There was much socializing privately, and a sweet custom of the day was to offer guests a spoon of jam with a glass of water as soon as they arrived and greeted their hosts.

I was also an inquisitive child and remember, for example, being particularly impressed by a young music teacher and wondering why she had become a nun because she was so pretty. I also had a tendency to question the political mores of the times. Anti-semitism in Romania was on the rise (two consecutive political regimes in the 1930s were anti-semitic). Since my family was Jewish (though non-practicing), those of us who attended the Catholic school were advised by the director to keep a low profile. Many of my questions were therefore discussed privately at home with my parents, and I focused on other things.

Blessed by a vivid imagination, I began to develop an intense passion for countries far beyond the borders of Romania. Reading the newspapers one day, I discovered an article about the 1939 World's Fair, which was soon to take place in New York City. I became obsessed with this event and pestered my parents repeatedly to take a trip to the United States to visit the fair. In my mind, it looked extraordinary. Henry David Thoreau once said, "Live the life you've imagined," and I was more than determined to follow this motto. Since I was their precious (and somewhat spoiled) daughter, my parents eventually acquiesced. They also made two important decisions that would alter the course of our lives: Not only would we visit the World's Fair, we would move to the United States permanently.

My father was, in fact, already thinking about leaving Bucharest. He had been working for a shipping company that offered travel from Hamburg, Germany, to destinations in South America. Its headquarters were in Hamburg, and because of poor economic conditions in Germany at that time, the company was forced to close, leaving my father out of work. In addition, the political situation in Romania was also rapidly changing: An ultra-nationalist, fascist movement led by an organization called the Iron Guard had been growing throughout the country since 1927. Though antisemitic laws already existed in the 1800s (Jews, for example, were urged to convert to Orthodox Christianity), they were greatly expanded in the 1930s and 1940s. As elsewhere in Europe, persecution of all types became the norm, eventually leading to the Holocaust. Jews were required to register their religion with the authorities and were not permitted to become Romanian citizens. As a result, we retained our Russian passports, and it is with these passports that we entered the United States in 1939.

Our departure proved to be fortuitous. Almost a year after we left, reinforcements of Hitler's army marched into Romania under the pretext of protecting important oil reserves and preparing an eastern base of operations against the Soviet Union. Had we stayed, we might have been among the 300,000 Romanian Jews and gypsies who were eventually deported to the concentration camps.

In the meantime, I was satisfied knowing it was my insistence to see the World's Fair that finally pushed my parents to make this critical decision – and probably saved our lives. I

At 16, just before
leaving Romania

Close friends seeing us off at the Bucharest train station,
with my parents at the window, Spring 1939

was 16 years old and ready to see the world, even though I knew I would be leaving my friends behind, especially Titel. A brother of my father's had been living in Chicago for many years, and he offered to help us out for a while. Since we had Russian passports, and there weren't many Russians leaving the Soviet Union at that time, we were able to enter the United States rather easily under the Russian quota. And we didn't have to pass through Ellis Island, as so many people were required to do decades earlier.

Fifteen of my parents' closest friends saw us off at the train station in Bucharest. The parting was bittersweet, knowing that we would probably not see each other again (though I would catch up with Titel years later in Israel), but I could hardly contain my own excitement at coming to a new country like the United States and moving there! We made the decision first to go to Paris, with a stop in Trieste, Italy, and then to Cherbourg on the west coast of France, where we would sail on the famous SS *Isle-de-France* for New York. This would be my first trip to Paris, the City of Lights.

In Paris, we bumped into friends of my parents who, coincidentally, were there at the

Bucharest street scene with the CEC Bank
in the background, late 1930s

View of the Champs Elysées (left) and
Avenue Marceau (right), early 1940s

same time. To a teenager like myself, the city was a vision from another planet – and simply gorgeous! Elegant architecture, monuments, and sculptures everywhere; wide boulevards teeming with people, buses, and the latest European and American cars (including Cadillacs!); fashionable women wearing beautiful hats and accessories; outdoor markets selling exquisite cheeses, pastries, and flowers; couples kissing on the Seine riverbanks; cafés and brasseries filled with loud chatter. I recall walking with my friends down the Champs Elysées, past a store with a lovely display of shoes behind a concave glass window. The shoes simply begged you to reach inside and place them on your feet… I also remember our friends inviting me to an afternoon tea dance, quite popular in those days, especially with young people. Paris in the spring of 1939 was a city pulsating with energy, completely oblivious to the dangers that lay ahead. The trip was wonderful, but I was more than ever looking forward to the rest of our journey.

Crossing the Atlantic from Cherbourg to New York in March of 1939 took six days, and our trip was rough and stormy the entire voyage. The *Isle-de-France* was a luxurious French ocean liner, the first to be entirely decorated in the Art Deco style. Built in 1927, it was especially popular with Americans and able to carry more than 1,500 passengers between Europe and the United States. It had made its first trip to New York from Le Havre, France, in 1927, and would be the last passenger ship to leave France in September 1939, just before the outbreak of World War II. During the war, it was gutted and used as a military vessel by the British Navy, then briefly rebuilt as a passenger ship that, in 1956, would help rescue more than 700 people from the sinking *Andrea Doria* when it collided with the MS *Stockholm* off the coast of Nantucket. This venerable ship would eventually be sold to a Japanese company, and be completely dismantled.

At the time of our trans-Atlantic crossing, however, the *Isle-de-France* was in its hey-day, and included a state-of-the-art dining-room, a four-level foyer, cabins with comfortable beds throughout the ship and a gym with all types of games. Given the poor weather conditions, we adjusted as best we could: My father, who liked to gamble, played poker on tables that would slide across smoke-filled rooms, while my mother became so ill with seasickness, she was given morphine injections, and spent the entire trip in bed. For some reason, this last detail remained imbedded in my mind because morphine seemed like such an odd remedy to me. I managed to be just fine, and though occasionally feeling queasy myself, passed the time playing shuffleboard, watching my father play poker, and attending to my mother.

The SS *Isle de France* ocean liner arriving into port

2. New York

Our first six months in America were spent in Chicago, living in the apartment of my uncle Manny, and his wife, Liza. Manny, who had been running a successful haberdashery in the city selling shirts, ties, and gloves, introduced my father to friends in the garment industry. While he was able to earn a small wage, my father did not adjust easily to life in the United States. He didn't like the feeling of being dependent on my uncle and was still unfamiliar with the English language. Frustrated, he began to think about returning to Bucharest, but once World War II broke out in Europe in September 1939, he dropped all intentions of going back.

In November 1940, Romania joined the Axis Alliance with Germany, Italy, and Japan and, though King Carol II, Romania's reigning monarch, was able at first to remain neutral, he was forced to abdicate under pressure from the Nazis. Fortunately, we were already in the United States, slowly adjusting to our adopted country. After a summer studying English in Chicago, we moved to Brooklyn, New York and settled in Brighton Beach, two blocks from the boardwalk and a short subway ride from Coney Island. Made famous by Neil Simon's hit play,

Poster, 1939 World's Fair, New York

General Motors *Diorama* exhibit, New York 1939 World's Fair

Brighton Beach Memoirs, this community had been a seaside destination for the wealthy through the 1930s. After the war, it slowly morphed into a predominantly Jewish neighborhood, filled with new immigrants from Europe – many of them Holocaust survivors. In the 1970s, it would transform itself again, this time into a mostly Russian-Ukrainian enclave that became known as "Little Odessa." Since the break-up of the Soviet Union, Brighton Beach has, more recently, also attracted people from Georgia, Armenia, and Uzbekistan – making it a very vibrant district in New York City.

As a New Yorker, my father again found a job buying and selling textiles, while my mother worked part-time assisting the elderly. I attended Abraham Lincoln High School and was on my way to becoming a true American. As planned, we did visit the "World of Tomorrow" World's Fair Exhibition in New York, and I remember thoroughly enjoying the vast array of international pavilions, especially two huge exhibits: the Consolidated Edison Company's City of Light, known as the "World's Largest Diorama" – which featured an exact miniature reproduction of Manhattan, with thousands of buildings and skyscrapers lighting up at night over an entire city block; and the impressive General Motors Futurama exhibit designed by Norman Bel Geddes, which, in 1939, was the first to introduce the public to the idea of an interconnected national highway system. With over a million components displayed at the fair across an acre-sized lot, the Futurama exhibit included replicas of everything from towns, buildings, and cars, to interstate roads, power plants, and farms. The concept of connecting roadways would eventually be implemented in 1960, and revolutionize ground transportation throughout the United States.

The best part of the trip for me, however, was our stay in the city of New York itself. What impressed me the most was the height of its skyscrapers, the friendliness of its people, and the vast number of theaters heralding one production after another around the theater district. Above all, it was in Manhattan that I was first introduced to American theater, with a program that included both a movie and a stage show, and was popular in those days. In my case, it was a Frank Sinatra movie, followed by the Duke Ellington band.

The Theater District was where I also saw my first Broadway musical, *Lady in the Dark*, starring the famous British singer/actress Gertrude

Typical 1940s movie and stage show, Paramount Theatre, Broadway

Actress Gertrude Lawrence in the 1941 musical, *Lady in the Dark*

High school graduation, May 1940

Spanish class, Brooklyn College,
New York

Lawrence. With music by Kurt Weill, and lyrics by Ira Gershwin, it was based on the emerging field of psychoanalysis (Sigmund Freud had recently died) and told the story of a fashion editor who learns to overcome panic attacks and depression through dream analysis – one of the cornerstones of Freudian psychology – with the help of a psychoanalyst. The play made such an impression on me that I later decided to major in psychology at what would become my alma mater, Barnard College.

In the meantime I still had to finish high school – which I was able to do in a year and a half at the age of 17. I had already taken so many advanced courses in Romania that they were readily accepted by the New York school system. Since I was younger than most, I put college on hold for a while, and instead decided to attend business school at night which, at that time, offered typing, shorthand, and basic business writing – skills that could be helpful in finding a job. Evening classes of two additional romance languages – Spanish and Portuguese – at Brooklyn College soon followed. The choice to delay college for a year would later prove valuable to my career as a producer: typing would always come in handy, and the business writing classes would help me hone my writing skills in English. And learning two additional languages would also become valuable assets.

Family portrait with my future husband, Oscar,
and my parents, Liza and David

OFFICE OF THE COORDINATOR
OF
INTER-AMERICAN AFFAIRS
1940—1944
OFFICE OF INTER-AMERICAN AFFAIRS
WASHINGTON, D.C.

WAR SERVICE CERTIFICATE

The Coordinator of Inter-American Affairs
and
The Director of the Office of Inter-American Affairs
hereby extend to

Eva Fields Maze

their grateful acknowledgement and appreciation
of the loyal and valued services rendered
during the war years while serving as
a member of the official staff.

War Service Certificate from Nelson
Rockefeller and the Office of
Inter-American Affairs

Looking back, these were smart decisions that I made as a young woman: They would have a positive effect on my future, and like pieces of a jigsaw puzzle, slowly help shape the picture of what would become a very fulfilling life.

During the day, I continued to live at home with my parents, and took several small jobs – one, as a secretary for a shipping company, and another, as a counselor for the Manhattan Beach Day Camp. I then found a wonderful position as a translator for the Office of the Coordinator of Inter-American Affairs. An agency of the State Department set up in 1940 under President Franklin D. Roosevelt's Good Neighbor Policy toward Latin America, it was headed by Nelson Rockefeller. Its main mission was to distribute news, advertising, film, and radio broadcasts throughout South America that counteracted propaganda fueled by the Germans and other Axis powers in that region. Materials were censored and designed to affect public opinion, and Latin-American businesses were encouraged – through financial incentives – to work with American companies. Hollywood institutions, such as the Walt Disney Company, were also asked to produce movies that would change the American public's perception of Latin American stereotypes. I spent one year working in their radio broadcast division on two regular programs, "Magazine of the Air" (Magazine do Ar) and "Brazil's Hour" (Hora do Brasil), translating Portuguese scripts about life in Brazil that originated in the Brazilian sector of the agency, into English. These texts were then vetted and broadcast throughout Brazil. While my Portuguese wasn't perfect, it was proficient enough for this job.

At the age of 18, I also had my first big crush on a much older man – an elegant 35-year-old Brazilian radio commentator with a beautiful voice, Irineo Macedo Soares, who worked in the same department as I did. Nothing romantic ever came out of this infatuation, but he did end up playing a crucial role in my life one evening when he invited me to a Russian War Relief dance. I don't know what would have happened had I refused to accompany him, but my life would have certainly followed a different path. For, in accepting his invitation, I was introduced to the man who would become my husband, Oscar Maze. At the time, Oscar was a handsome, young 24-year-old Air Force private stationed on Governor's Island, New York. He asked me out to dinner, and to a show at Carnegie Hall that was featuring the famous Spanish flamenco dancer, Carmen Amaya. With my European upbringing, I was surprised at how much he knew about the arts, and his invitation made quite an impression on me. He also looked dashing in his Air Force uniform and, as someone who was sensitive to music and sound, I found myself attracted to his voice, which had a lovely, deep radio-like resonance to it. We started seeing each other more often, and I learned that he had lived in Mexico for six months, studied Spanish there, and was interested in joining the diplomatic corps when the war was over.

Oscar was the youngest of four siblings – two brothers and a sister – and his family had originally come from Poland at the turn of the century through Ellis Island. His parents, Ethel and Joseph Mazursky, lived near Princeton, New Jersey, and the children had changed their names to Maze. His older brother, Howard, ran a country store in Jamesburg, New Jersey, with his father. His other brother, Alvin, had joined the Army and become a successful dentist, graduating

Our wedding day, Sunday, December 27, 1942, Brooklyn, New York

from the University of Pennsylvania. Alvin's son, Barry, would follow suit after graduating from Duke, settling down as a dentist in Jamesburg, New Jersey. His sister, Pearl, was an activist for women's causes who would later marry a pioneer in the field of developmental disabilities, Dr. Bert MacLeech. An early advocate of community-based services for young handicapped people in the 1950s, and a Harvard graduate who became a professor of special education at the University of Southern California, he and Pearl would go on to found the Young Adult Institute (YAI) in New York City. Launched in 1957, and housing several youths in their late teens, its mission was to keep young people with developmental disabilities out of institutions, and integrate them into the community. The program eventually grew into the National Institute for People with Disabilities, that now serves more than 20,000 people (and their families) with 500 programs daily in New York City, Puerto Rico, and the Virgin Islands.

Oscar and I shared many common interests, and after a six–month courtship, he proposed to me in writing with a very charming letter, and I happily accepted. We were married in New York City in December 1942. He was a private first class in the United States Air Force, and I, a 20-year old, part-time student. My parents thought I was too young to marry, but times were different during the war. The future was uncertain and no one knew what would or could happen.

In fact, soon after we were married – and a short winter honeymoon in Lake Placid, N.Y., where we both learned to ski – Oscar was sent to the Air Force Officer Training School in Iowa. He had been moving up in rank in the Air Force, and I recall how proud he was to come back to New York as a second lieutenant. We had a rendezvous at the Park Central Hotel in Manhattan, and I remember his face beaming with joy now that he had become an officer.

The Air Force began sending him to different airports around the United States. Albuquerque, New Mexico, was his next assignment, and I joined him there. On my way to Albuquerque, I stopped in Chicago to replenish my wardrobe at Marshall Field's. I didn't know much about the store, but, with my European sense of style, was determined to buy appropriate clothes for what I imagined would be a Western lifestyle – complete with jodhpurs, boots, and a suede jacket with fringes. My outfits did come in handy in Albuquerque as I learned to ride horses, but I soon found out that regular clothes worked best for most occasions. Oscar was very athletic and, in addition to skiing (and later tennis), he also taught me to ride. We would take horseback rides together along the famous Rio Grande, which – much to my disappointment – was completely dry at that time.

Our stay in Albuquerque was short, and my husband was soon transferred to Pittsburgh, Pennsylvania. I was in the process of applying to the University of New Mexico, but when Oscar was relocated, changed my application to the University of Pittsburgh, with the idea of pursuing a college degree there. The campus was lovely, and in registering for my courses – philosophy, logic, and history of Latin America, among others – I was surprised to see a tall skyscraper appear out of nowhere. With its cathedral-like shape and grandeur, it stood out in sharp contrast to the other low buildings on campus. Called the Cathedral of Learning – and later added as a landmark to the National Register of Historic Places – it was built in the style of Gothic Revival, and housed the Administrative Offices of the university. It also featured a number of rooms called "Nationality Rooms" – each one furnished according to the style of a particular country. They reminded me of the pavilions at the World's Fair.

It was then, at the age of 20 that I also returned to my former great love – ballet – and began taking the ballet classes I had so yearned for as a young child.

I found a very good teacher – Frank Eckl, Director of the Pittsburgh Ballet and father of Shirley Eckl, who was one of the original dancers in the American Ballet Theatre's production of

Cathedral of Learning building,
University of Pittsburgh

Student portrait at the
University of Pittsburgh

31

Flamenco dance with the Pittsburgh Ballet, 1944

Jerome Robbins' *Fancy Free.* Taking class only once a week, I did well enough to be given a solo part in the school's annual concert. Since I was starting ballet at such an advanced age, Mr. Eckl suggested I study character dance, which was a bit easier to master. In the repertoire of large, classical ballets, there are always short dances that reflect the folk character of a particular country, and because of my age, he thought I would be a good fit for this type of dance. I was assigned a Spanish dance for the concert, and as Shirley Eckl was helping her father prepare for the concert, she also worked with me on my footwork and overall style.

Finally, in 1942, I made my official stage debut as a dancer with the Pittsburgh Ballet at Pittsburgh's Carnegie Hall. My solo was well received, and I was thrilled, but this, too, proved to be short-lived: As I was rehearsing and taking class in Pennsylvania, Oscar was offered a temporary position by Pan American Airways at La Guardia Airport in New York. Assigned to what was known as "dispatch," he was asked to help prepare and coordinate, for the pilots, all aspects of an airplane's flight prior to takeoff: flight plan, load, fuel, food, weather, crew, passengers on board, etc. Deciding to stay behind in Pittsburgh to finish my academic year and ballet performances, I came to the conclusion that I needed a college degree. I also realized that, regardless of whether I performed on stage or not in the future, I had found that missing link in my life that would always make me feel good: studying ballet and being involved with dance. And, as a partner who valued initiative and creativity in others – especially with women – I knew Oscar would be there to cheer me on. I then joined my husband in New York City and, changing colleges once again, was accepted by Columbia University, where I would enter Barnard College.

Soon after arriving in New York, I lost no time looking for a good ballet school. With a recommendation from Frank Eckl, I found my way to the Steinway Hall Building on 57th Street, which housed the studio of Ludmilla Schollar and her husband, Anatole Vilzak. As I entered the building, I kept telling myself how lucky I was to be there. I was desperately hoping to be able to take classes with this legendary couple, knowing that they had both danced with the original Ballets Russes company under the direction of impresario Sergei Diaghilev. The Paris-based Ballets Russes and his troupe of classically trained Russian dancers had performed to great acclaim all over Europe and the Americas between 1909-1929. Considered by many as one of the world's most influential ballet companies of the 20th century, it had brought together some of the most creative choreographers and superbly trained dancers of the day, including Michel Fokine, Vaslav Nijinsky, Léonide Massine, and a young George Balanchine – as well as artists such as Pablo Picasso, Henri Matisse, and Joan Miró, and composers Claude Debussy, Sergei Prokofiev, and Igor Stravinsky.

Sitting in the small reception area, I remember how excited I was as I waited to meet them. My heart was pounding with anticipation as I heard the familiar strains of ballet music on a rehearsal piano behind the studio's closed door. There was a desk, but no secretary, so I waited. As the music stopped a dancer, who looked vaguely familiar, emerged from the room and headed down a narrow hallway, perspiration running down her back after what seemed to have been an intensive, privately coached session. A moment later, a short, rotund woman walked out of the classroom and came up to me.

"Yes?" she said loudly, with a strong Russian accent, scrutinizing me from head to toe.

"Are you here for ballet classes?"

At first, I was startled because hearing her speak reminded me of my first ballet teacher in Bucharest, Madame Semeonova, so much so that she could have easily been her twin. I knew, of course, that this was the famous Ludmilla Schollar, former ballerina with the Kirov Ballet who had once danced with the great Nijinsky.

"Yes. I am," I answered, my voice barely above a whisper.

"And your training?" she asked, adding, "You're not a child… I don't know where to place you… Tell me about yourself."

Though normally outspoken and rarely shy, I had to pause for a moment. Her direct, almost rude manner of speaking seemed so familiar I thought, for a brief moment, I was back in Bucharest.

"I'm a student at Barnard College, majoring in psychology, but my passion is dance, especially classical ballet. I am also taking some required classes in contemporary dance in college. I know I'm an adult, and that I won't be a classical dancer in any ballet company, but I just moved here from Pittsburgh where I was studying with Frank Eckl, and recently had some success performing a Spanish dance solo at their yearly concert."

"Hmm," she murmured. "You're not the only one like that in New York City. There always seem to be students who study as children, then they stop…. But I detect an accent… You weren't born here…."

"No, Bucharest…."

"And you didn't study as a child."

"I started to, but then had an illness…."

"At least, you're honest…can you arrange to take some private classes? Then I'll see… and maybe we can put you in the evening class with my husband," she added, her tone softening a bit as she noticed how delighted I was to follow her suggestion.

This was to be the beginning of a very long friendship…

After taking several private lessons with her, I joined her husband's evening class that included a combination of beginners, amateurs, and professional dancers. The atmosphere in these sessions was exhilarating. I loved every minute and couldn't wait to get to the next class.

With my academic classes in full swing at Barnard – as well as my ballet classes – I had a full schedule. I found the modern dance programs offered at Barnard as part of my courses to be intriguing, and signed up for classes with Nina Fonaroff, a former dancer with the Martha Graham Company. It was an exciting time for modern dance, and Martha Graham's company was beginning to receive the attention it deserved beyond the insular avant-garde coteries of the day. A unique radio show with a large audience at the time called "Hush" – where the listeners had to call in to identify different voices and music – helped to promote Graham's name further. On one such program, she herself became "Miss Hush," reading a short essay based on the familiar Christmas poem, "The Night Before Christmas." People listening were supposed to guess who she was. Once they called in after she finished, Martha Graham would invite them to attend one of her shows, usually held at a New York City high school. At the time, she was in her early forties, and her performances were attended by either a small, elite group of New Yorkers interested in the arts, or by other dancers.

Martha Graham had formed her own company in 1926, and invented an entirely new language in modern dance, character-ized by forceful movements designed to symbolize emotional turmoil. Her influence was felt far and wide during her 70 years as a dancer and choreographer, and has lasted long after her death at the age of 96 in 1991. It has also helped launch other famous contem-porary dancers, such as Merce Cunningham, Paul Taylor, Erick Hawkins, Anna Sokolow, and Yuriko.

Martha Graham on NBC's
Miss Hush radio program

Graham dancing in Aaron Copeland's
Appalachian Spring

In college, modern dance was taught for many years under the physical education departments. Only in later years – long after I had graduated from Barnard – was dance finally recognized as a separate department at American colleges and universities. In my case, these modern dance classes gave me a strong educational foundation in contemporary dance, one that would prove invaluable in later years as I began to sponsor modern dance tours of companies such as the Alvin Ailey American Dance Theater, José Limón, and Lar Lubovitch.

At Barnard, I also joined a group of students who were studying dance composition (i.e. choreography) with Louis Horst, a well-known professor at the college. Horst was a real character, and I use the word "character" by choice. At the time, he must have been in his mid-sixties, but to me, he seemed like an old man. He had been Martha Graham's mentor since her early days in California and was still advising her. He was also founder and editor of the influential Dance Observer – the first magazine of its kind to feature dance criticism and theory – and as such, was in the unique position of commenting on a student's talents in choreography. A rigorous disciplinarian, who at times made young students cry, Horst rarely smiled, and nothing escaped his penetrating eye. In class, he would hover over the keyboard, a cigarette dangling from his mouth, growling comments at you as you demonstrated your choreographic ability with a short dance sequence. He was a firm believer in structure and taught a type of dance composition that was based on dance forms of the 16th and 17th century Renaissance – such as the Pavane and the Galliard. His modern dance techniques went on to influence scores of famous choreographers and dancers, including Doris Humphrey, José Limón, Ruth Page, Paul Taylor, and Merce Cunningham.

Learning from Horst, I based the choreography of my own class projects on his lectures about different rhythms, and used them as a basis for matching movement to various tempos. It was my first experience with choreography and, at a concert at the MacMillan Theatre on the Columbia campus, a group of four Barnard women – myself included, along with Leora Dana (who became a well-known Broadway actress) – performed the interpretative dance of a dying flower that I had choreographed. Fortunately, it was well received.

My years at Barnard College were stimulating, and I was like a sponge, absorbing anything that came my way. I also enrolled in a course on radio program directing. With my previous interest in radio, and the experience I gained while working with the Brazilian radio

Representing Barnard College for the United Nations Student Association (front row, seated in a striped shirt), along with students from other universities

producer before my marriage, this was an opportunity to learn more about this field. Little did I know then that my professional future would, among others, include creating radio programs in New Delhi, India. While taking this course at Columbia, I ended up producing for UCRC – the Columbia University radio station – a dramatized program about cultural differences of a variety of countries around the world. This led to a brief involvement with the United Nations Student Organization, then located at Lake Success, NY, and to my becoming its United States student director for the greater New York area. When I later moved to England, I would again represent this organization at a seminar in Loch Lomond, Scotland, as part of a national student group from the United States.

Shortly after World War II came to a close, my husband, who was still with the Air Force, was offered a permanent position with Pan American Airways, which he accepted in 1946. He had always wanted to become a pilot, but because of sub-standard eyesight and the fact that

Beginning of Pan American World Airways' flight service in 1927

Pan American Airways System poster with the first of four types of flying boats, the Sikorsky S-40 Flying Clipper, which began operating in 1931

he wore glasses, this was not an option. Instead, he opted to join the company's burgeoning flight operations division, where he would oversee the departure and arrival of every type of aircraft in Pan Am's fleet around the world for the next 45 years. He would become known throughout the company as one of the best in his field (a "legend" by some) right up to his death in 1992. Deeply respectful of the military, he also chose to remain with the Air Force Reserve until the end of his life, completing all of his military requirements around Europe each year, and, in addition to his responsibilities within Pan Am, would eventually reach the rank of Lt. Colonel in the Reserve.

In 1946, however, mass commercial air travel was still in its infancy. Originally founded in 1929 as a small airmail and passenger flying-boat service between Key West, Florida, and Havana, Cuba, Pan American Airways (PAA) soon expanded its seaplane service into Central and South America, Europe, and Asia, using a fleet of Sikorsky and Boeing flying boats known as "Clippers." These seaplanes would eventually carry up to 74 passengers and a crew of 11, and include 36 seats that could change into sleeping bunks. The crews had to undergo

Pan American Airways Sikorsky S-42 Flying Boat taking-off from Miami in 1934. Used for
the South American routes – and as survey flights over the Pacific – it averaged 157.5 miles per hour,
set new speed, payload, and altitude records, and cut travel time by almost half.

intensive training in long-distance flying, sea navigation, seaplane anchoring, marine tides, radio communication, and aircraft repair. They became known for wearing military-style uniforms and marching in specific order as they boarded the planes. Later, with the advent of land aircraft, they would line up along the stairs and salute the captain as he entered the aircraft.

By the time Oscar joined the company in 1946, Pan Am was upgrading its fleet, expanding its routes into Asia and Europe, and facing growing competition from other airlines, including Trans World Airlines (TWA), and United Airlines. Pressurized land aircraft such as the Lockheed Constellation and the Douglas DC4s had replaced the flying boats, and the first regular landplane flights had begun to cross the Atlantic. In 1946, travel time on a DC4 from New York's LaGuardia Airport to London's Heathrow Airport, for example, took 17 hours and 40 minutes, and Pan Am started seven of these flights a week. In June 1947, the company also initiated the first round-the-world flights, which included several plane changes. So Oscar was pretty busy when he learned about his first overseas assignment in 1948 to London's Heathrow airport in England.

This meant that we would be living in London for several years, and I would need to wrap up my studies quickly at Barnard before joining him. So I doubled down on my classes and went to summer school. I remember studying on the grassy banks of Riverside Drive, feeling so much pressure, I thought I was going to have a nervous breakdown. Persevering to the end, I finally graduated from college and received my degree from Columbia University in February 1947.

As I said goodbye to Madame Schollar before joining my husband in London, she not only reminded me that she thought I could become a good character dancer if I chose to do so, she also suggested that I continue my ballet training at the studio of Vera Volkova, a well-known ballet teacher in London. Volkova had emigrated from Russia and trained under another famous Russian ballet instructor, Agrippina Vaganova, who had perfected a system of classical ballet instruction at the school of the Imperial Ballet – later known as the Kirov Ballet – of St. Petersburg, Russia.

In exchange, I promised to call her whenever I visited New York.

Pan Am's *Flying Cloud* Boeing Stratocruiser landing at Heathrow Airport,
England, on its first 1949 transatlantic flight from Gander, Newfoundland

3. London

According to Pan Am, London was considered a "hardship" post in 1948. The airline was in its early stages of development, and the city had been heavily destroyed by the relentless bombing of the Germans during the September 1940 to May 1941 Blitz. A number of streets remained pockmarked by craters, and rubble kept piling up between the shattered buildings. The games of the XIVth Olympiad – originally scheduled for 1944 in London, but cancelled because of the war – were eventually held in 1948, and became known as the "Austerity Games."

My husband flew to London ahead of me as I finished my last semester at Barnard, and I soon followed. Upon my arrival, I was surprised to find Oscar sharing an apartment with a Pan Am colleague on Half Moon Street in the Piccadilly district, then known as an area of prostitution. We quickly looked for another apartment, and in fact moved three more times before finally settling into a small townhouse in Wimbledon on the outskirts of the city.

Though London was still reeling from all the damage, and strict rationing of food and other goods was the norm of daily life, I loved every minute of the few years we lived there.

Food ration lines, London, England, 1948 (top);
Piccadilly Circle, London, early 1950s (left); and the
view from our Wimbledon Hill Road home (above)

The city was an exciting place to be for a ballet enthusiast like me, and I soon became aware of two remarkable women who were re-inventing ballet in England at the time: Dame Ninnette de Valois and Dame Marie Rambert, both of whom had been associated with Sergei Diaghiliev and the Ballets Russes company in its early years. Dame Ninnette de Valois had since formed the Vic-Wells Company, which had now grown into the Sadler's Wells Company. It would eventually become the Royal Ballet under a royal charter. Choreographer Frederick Ashton – later known as Sir Frederick Ashton – was hard at work creating an impressive list of ballets for this young Sadler's Wells Company. Many of his works would become classics, such as *La Fille Mal Gardée*, *Sleeping Beauty*, and *Les Patineurs*, and his repertoire would eventually include close to one hundred ballets.

Dame Marie Rambert was known for the famed Ballet Rambert, which she had success-fully molded from a small ballet school founded in 1920 into Britain's oldest dance company. Along with Dame Ninette de Valois, she nurtured Frederick Ashton's work during his first for-ays into the world of classical ballet. She did the same with one of her other protégés, Antony Tudor, creator of the classic *Jardin aux Lilas* and *Dark Elegies*, two well-known ballets originally choreographed for the Ballet Rambert that are still performed to this day. Ballet Rambert's home became the Mercury Theatre, and a magnet for a variety of talented young dancers and choreog-raphers during the pre- to post-war years. The company developed a loyal audience – especially after it was featured in the movie *The Red Shoes*, starring dancer-actress Moira Shearer.

Following up on Madame Schollar's advice to contact friends of hers in London, I soon made my way to a dance studio on West Street in the city's West End, and introduced myself to two very influential Russian ballet teachers, Vera Volkova and George Goncharov. They had been former dancers themselves, had spent time in China and Cuba as ballet instructors, and had taught for years in London at the Sadler's Wells Ballet. Both were very Russian in style: extremely precise and demanding of a dancer's posture, strict disciplinarians, and classical ballet traditionalists. They were highly sought out as teachers, and a number of famous ballet stars worked with them.

Before leaving New York, I had advanced to pointe (toe) work and adagio (pas-de-deux) dancing with a partner and felt confident enough to sign up for classes there. That self-assurance was momentarily shaken, however, when I came face to face with some of the

Dame Ninette de Valois in Frederick Ashton's *A Wedding Bouquet*

Dame Margot Fonteyn in Sir Frederick Ashton's *Birthday Offering*

Actress-ballerina Moira Shearer after her success in *The Red Shoes*

other big names who were training at the studio then: the now famous Moira Shearer; the very elegant and always polite Margot Fonteyn; the very dashing Erik Bruhn, lead dancer of the Royal Danish Ballet; and two wonderful soloists with the Royal Ballet, Beryl Grey and Alexander Grant. With many other well-known Sadler's Wells Ballet dancers popping in and out of the studio at any time, there was never a dull moment.

I began adapting to my new surroundings, and they soon felt like a second home. Many ballet stars and professional dancers had trained with Madame Volkova, and though a bit daunting, I didn't feel strange or out of place in their classes. I had become accustomed to ballet studios in Pittsburgh and New York, and come to realize that all studios, regardless of their locations, convey a similar sense of familiarity. It seems to kick in automatically as soon as you enter the room and begin to dance, whether it's your first time there or not.

The studio in London was no exception. There was that unfailing musty smell that seems to welcome you in any ballet studio – a combination of sweat and perfume that emanates from the dancers' bodies as they warm up on the floor or over the barres. There was also that similar physical layout to each classroom: one wall, lined with mirrors for dancers to rehearse choreography, and continuously evaluate body positions and lines; another, equipped with ballet barres, used for the warm-up exercises of pliés, port-de-bras, developés, and jetés – among many other ballet positions. An upright piano usually stood in the corner of the room, with a live piano accompanist playing familiar excerpts from ballet classics that are designed to motivate dancers to push their bodies to their maximum potential. The position of every limb, scrutinized by the ever-critical eye of the instructor (and the dancers themselves), must meet all the strict rules established by this demanding dance form. While I, at first, did feel a bit intimidated by the professional dance level of the classes, I soon began to relax and enjoy the atmosphere as I started taking class on a daily basis. So determined was I to attend class, I even managed to find my way to the studio on those famous London fog days when I couldn't see my fingers. With regular attendance, my comfort level continued to rise, and though I knew I would never become a prima ballerina, I did well enough in these sessions to feel I belonged there. Pickaniny ('Picky'), my miniature French poodle, who went everywhere with me, and was allowed into the studio, seemed to feel the same way. On one occasion, he made his own mark on the dance floor by peeing on it – much to my embarrassment (the instructor and dancers just laughed). As my self-confidence grew, so did my desire to try-out for minor parts, and I

Walking to ballet class with my poodle "Picky"

Dancing in the Volkova-Goncharov London ballet studio

began auditioning for several American musicals that were popular in London at the time. I received several callbacks for shows like *Carousel* and *High Button Shoes*, and was almost hired for the ballet corps, until I learned I was passed over because I didn't have the right work visa. On my third audition – this time as a corps dancer for a television program about ballet – I just decided to say I was English, and no one questioned me further. I got the job and, as a result of that engagement, was hired for two more productions – televised operas – one as a mime in *Tales of Hoffman*, and the other as a street sweeper in *La Bohème*.

Personally, I was delighted with the opportunity to perform professionally, but some of the other dancers weren't too thrilled about it. They questioned my motives for auditioning for parts they claimed took work away from them. After all, I was married, and married women in those days were deemed to be supported by their husband, and therefore not to be needing as much money as single wage-earners. I told them that professional recognition was important to me and that, as a dancer, I wanted to be paid for my work. I felt that, even though I had begun to study ballet late in life, being selected for small parts not only boosted my self-esteem and self-validation as a dancer, it also encouraged me –

Performing as an extra in the BBC television opera production of *La Bohème*

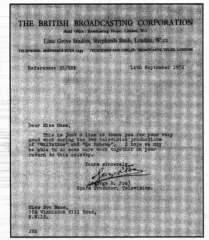

Letter from BBC opera producer, George Foa, on our move to India

47

with Oscar's loyal support – to keep auditioning for more parts.

These performances, however, were short-lived. I soon learned I was pregnant, and three months later, had to stop dancing. Then, upon returning to London after giving birth to my daughter, Stephanie, in New York, Oscar informed me we were being transferred to a new location within six months: New Delhi, India.

While I didn't know what to expect in India – and was a bit apprehensive about the move – the idea of venturing out into an entirely new and mysterious world intrigued me. After two and a half years of London life, I had, on some level, become tired of the bleakness of bombed-out buildings and food rations, and was content to leave them behind. I also felt I would be able to continue some form of ballet training at my next destination.

With my one-year-old daughter, Stephanie

4. New Delhi

I had once attended a performance of Indian dance in New York City and at the time found it fascinating. Yet it was not until we were transferred to New Delhi, India, that I began to understand and truly appreciate this intricate and captivating dance form, and its different styles. I had no idea India would also mark a turning point in my life, and that it would be so varied and enriching.

From the time we landed in New Delhi in 1951 to the day we left for our next assignment in Frankfurt, Germany, in 1954, not a moment went by that didn't include either a surprise or an adventure. It was the beginning of a very creative period for me, filled with a host of new projects of my choosing. And I took advantage of every interesting opportunity that came my way.

Unlike London, where we had lived a relatively quiet and organized European middle-class life, first in a South Kensington apartment, then in a house in Wimbledon, New Delhi was quite the opposite: chaotic, dirty, noisy, hot, poor, and very exotic.

India at that time was in a state of momentous change. The turmoil of achieving final independence from Great Britain in 1948, inspired by Mahatma Gandhi and his movement of nonviolent disobedience, had also brought about what became known as "The Partition," dividing the country along religious lines into a Hindu-majority India and a Muslim-majority Pakistan. This caused an intense upheaval that led to the massacre of hundreds of thousands of people and displacement of close to 10 million. Shortly before our arrival in 1951, the newly elected head of state, President Rajendra Prasat, and Prime Minister Jawaharlal Nehru had formed India's first constitutional government, which helped usher in a period of stability. It is in this climate that we landed in New Delhi.

Housing in the capital in those days was scarce, and foreigners – mostly diplomats, journalists, writers, and business people – were assigned to hotels in an area of Old Delhi called the "Civil Lines." Known as the "Shahar" by the locals, the Civil Lines had originated under the British Raj (British rule) when Delhi was divided into civilian and military districts, and the Civil Lines district was designated for civilians. It was the hub of all major shopping (handicrafts, clothes, jewelry, spices, books, etc.) and included some of the best hotels in India. We lived in a posh Swiss-run hotel with over a hundred rooms, called the Hotel Cecil, on an elegant

Old Delhi 1950s street scenes of Chandni Chowk district, known for its market and
Majestic Cinema (left), and the area outside of Kashmir Gate (right)

enclave of more than eleven thousand acres set in a beautifully landscaped park. Known as the "Country Club" because of its manicured gardens, mahogany neem trees, beautiful flowers, and numerous amenities, it would later become the St. Xavier School of India, a Jesuit-run school for boys that is operating to this day.

In those early days, however, the residents of the Cecil had their own apartments, ate their meals in an elegant common dining room, and had their own servants. The custom then was to have butlers, cooks, chauffeurs, nannies, housekeepers, and even tailors (called "dirseys"). Though salaries were very low (pennies by today's standards) and paid on a daily basis, they supplemented the livelihood of many poor people. The jobs were specific: for example, there were "bearers"– a holdover from the British – who were responsible for dusting furniture, doing errands and babysitting in the evening, and "sweepers," who would be assigned to cleaning floors. We had a personal tailor who was paid the unbelievable price of 5 rupees a day (at a time when a dollar was worth 118 rupees) to sit at his sewing machine outside our door and create beautiful evening dresses for me, each one usually completed in two days.

This type of employment also forged strong bonds between hired help and the families

British five-star Hotel Cecil and its common dining hall, in the Delhi Civil Lines area, where we lived from 1951-1954. The hotel later became the Jesuit St. Xavier Senior Secondary School.

themselves. When it eventually came time for us to leave again for our next post in Frankfurt, Germany, we all cried together, especially our bearer Sonny, who wanted very much to come with us. A loyal man and very protective of my daughter, he would sit for hours outside our door waiting for us to give him errands, while an ayah (an Indian nanny) cared for my daughter, Stephanie, during the day. Stephanie's young nanny was a lovely Nepalese girl, and I remember how, for example, the small ring dangling from her nose fascinated my daughter.

New Delhi was the political center of the country, with a newly formed parliamentary system of government that represented all of the country's regions, and it was host to embassies from all over the world. Many of its ambassadors resided at the Cecil and nearby hotels in the Civil Lines region.

The world of the Cecil Hotel, with its fragrant gardens and deep blue swimming pool, was an island of calm unto itself, providing a welcome relief to the city's chaotic hustle and bustle. After a sweaty and exhausting day of dealing with the intensity of the capital, and negotiating everything from transportation to language to untouchable sacred cows, it always felt good to return to this oasis.

Curious about my new home, I became an avid reader of Indian political and cultural history and of the amazing variety of Indian classical dances, especially the Kathak, Kathakhali, Manipuri, and Bharatanatyam styles. I checked out the dance scene only to learn that classical ballet instruction was not to be found in the city, and decided instead to immerse myself in the study of Indian classical dance.

 After reading as much as I could find on the subject, I located several classes that were being offered by Rajendra Shankar, a younger brother of the well-known Indian dancer, Uday Shankar, who had worked for many years with Russian-born prima ballerina Anna Pavlova. The celebrated sitar player Ravi Shankar, who later became famous in the United States, was also a brother of his. I began with Bharatanatyam, the oldest and most traditional dance form in India, and also one of the country's original temple dances. Known for its angular poses and rapid eye and facial movements, Bharatanatyam originated in the south of India and is considered to be the pre-eminent style of Indian classical dance. I also immersed myself in Manipuri, a softer Indian dance form from northeast India that features more undulating movements. The Bharatanatyam style seemed more ornamental and stationary to me personally, and I related better to the Manipuri form, which offered freer-flowing movements across the floor.

I didn't find Indian dance difficult and seemed to follow the choreography without too much effort. Because of my previous ballet training, my body was flexible enough to adjust to the variety of poses. For this dance style, particularly with Bharatanatyam, one has to master many hand gestures, and, at the same time, follow different rhythmic beats designed specifically for the feet – so coordinating intricate footwork with upper body movement is essential. Indian dance usually portrays stories based on Hindu mythology, such as the legend of Ramayana and its Indian Emperor Bharata, who united India and, through song and movement, pays homage to revered Hindu gods, in particular Vishnu, the Supreme God of Hinduism, and his avatar Rama, symbol of chivalry and virtue.

Our social lives revolved around the international community at the Cecil. Filled with fascinating people, the hotel presented us with opportunities for some wonderful experiences. On one occasion, for example, the Nepalese ambassador to India, Vijaya Shumsher J.R. Rana, who had become a good friend of ours, invited us one evening to a dinner-dance party at the Imperial Hotel, then the finest hotel in New Delhi. When the orchestra began playing Latin

Rendering of a Bharatanatyam Indian dancer, by German artist Egon Chajewske

Delhi social life in the 1950s included polo tournaments, with winners posing for a photo with President Rajendra Prasad of India at the Delhi Gymkhana Club.

rhythms, one of the guests, King Tribhuvan Bir Bikram of Nepal, who was staying with the ambassador in New Delhi at the time, expressed an interest in learning to dance the samba. King Tribhuvan had recently returned to Nepal after spending some time in Switzerland. He had lived in exile there from 1950-1951 "under mysterious circumstances" that were attributed to a poor heart condition, but were in fact due to internal political conflicts. He and Prime Minister Jawahar Nehru of India had forged a close relationship.

Familiar with the Brazilian samba, I, of course, immediately offered to help the king, and as the orchestra continued to play, tapped out its rhythm for him with my foot. At the same time, my husband, Oscar, who was a good dancer in his own right, also invited one of the Nepalese princesses to dance with him, and showed her some samba moves as well. So here we were on the dance floor in India, teaching Nepalese royalty how to dance a Brazilian samba. This became one of my most endearing memories of India.

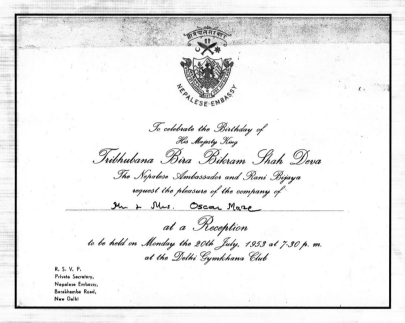

To celebrate the Birthday of
His Majesty King
Tribhubana Bira Bikram Shah Deva
The Nepalese Ambassador and Rani Bijaya
request the pleasure of the company of

Mr. & Mrs. Oscar Maze

at a Reception
to be held on Monday the 20th July, 1953 at 7-30 p. m.
at the Delhi Gymkhana Club

R. S. V. P.
Private Secretary,
Nepalese Embassy,
Barakhamba Road,
New Delhi

Invitation by Nepalese Ambassador Vijaya Shumsher J. B. Rana, in
honor of King Tribhuvan Bira Bikram Shah Deva's birthday

Ambassador Shumsher then arranged for my husband and me to visit Nepal. There was hardly any tourism in the country at that time, and, staying at an American diplomat's house, we essentially became guests of a transitional government that was shifting from a hundred-year dynasty under the Rana regime (1846-1951) to a new constitutional monarchy, established by King Tribhuvan Bir Bikram upon his return to Nepal in 1951. In addition, India and Nepal had signed the Treaty of Peace and Friendship in Kathmandu as recently as 1950. This, in turn, had opened up free trade and movement between both nations, and forged a close defense and diplomatic alliance along the "Himalayan Frontier" (India, Nepal, Sikkim, and Bhutan). Because of this treaty, India and Nepal were able to thwart a 1952 coup by the Communist Party of Nepal (founded in 1949) that was backed by the Chinese Communist Party.

Our arrival in Nepal in 1953 coincided with a number of these issues – as well as with tensions within various factions of the Rana family itself – and we were asked to be discreet. The ambassador, a member of one of the Rana families, personally helped us with our accommodations and introduced us to other members of the royal family. The Nepalese could not have been more gracious. Not only did the son of the defense minister of Nepal meet us at the airport: He also became our personal guide for our entire visit in Kathmandu. Pretty heady stuff for a young couple from Brooklyn!

Our stay in Nepal began with an invitation for dinner with the Royal Princesses, followed by a performance with Nepalese dancers from the Royal Court. A sightseeing tour on horseback was arranged the next day. Though my riding days in Albuquerque came in handy, the hilly trails there had sharp, vertical drops and, with the frisky horse I was given, the fear of falling was not far from my mind. Oscar, who never seemed frightened of anything, managed to calm me down, and eventually exchanged horses with me. The unpaved roads around Kathmandu were extremely narrow, and most people traveled on horseback – except for one of the young princes who preferred driving a bright yellow Buick convertible, which had been disassembled in the United States and re-assembled in Kathmandu. He would zoom around the ridiculously steep roads, proudly showing off his favorite toy.

During our ten days in Nepal, we also participated in the excitement surrounding Sir Edmund Hillary's ascent to the top of Mt. Everest. A native of New Zealand and an experienced climber, he became, on May 29, 1953, the first man ever to reach the summit and highest point on Earth. Hillary was part of a larger British expedition, and the day he and his Sherpa guide, Tenzing Norgay, reached Mt. Everest also coincided with the coronation day of Queen Elizabeth II. So there was much jubilation all over Kathmandu, and it was just by sheer luck that we happened to be there for both, celebrating along with everyone else! It is with great sadness that I recently learned – 62 years later – that so many of the quaint and lively towns we had visited then, have been destroyed by the 2015 earthquake.

Shortly after our experience in Nepal and Kathmandu, King Tribhuvan Bir Bikram returned to Switzerland, dying there several months later. His eldest grandson, Gyanendra Bir Bikram Shah became the new king, and his family remained in control of the country for a number of years. Kathmandu became a popular tourist destination, but political tensions within the royal family increased, ending with a horrible murder in 1956 that was never solved. After

Bargaining for gas, downtown Kathmandu

Villagers in Patan near Kathmandu

Burning and bathing Ghats along the Bagmati River

Temple Square, city of Bhatgaon

Street scene, center of Patan

Saying goodbye at Kathmandu Airport

View of the Himalayas and Mount Everest, Nepal,
from Darjeeling, India, October 1953

my husband was transferred to his next post in Frankfurt, Germany, we would sadly learn that our elegant and charming friend, Ambassador Vijaya Shumsher had been assassinated in an ongoing feud between rival members of the Rana family and the royal descendants of King Tribhuvan.

Back in New Delhi after our exhilarating trip to Nepal in 1953, Oscar and I returned to our routines – and horseback riding. Up at 4:00 a.m., we would saddle up two horses loaned to us by one of the sons of the owner of the Cecil Hotel and go for our morning excursion. On one such occasion, my horse decided to take off in a gallop, with me hanging on for dear life. Luckily, one of the bodyguards of India's president, Rajendra Prasad, who was training his own horse nearby, managed to stop him. It would be a long time before I would get back on a horse.

During this period, I also began a friendship with Khushwant Singh, the producer of "All India Radio" in New Delhi. A fascinating man – and a Sikh – who recently died at the age of 99, he was a lawyer, a diplomat, a journalist, an historian, and an author. We would have lengthy discussions about his book on India and religion, *The Mark of Vishnu and Other Stories*. A man who was very committed to his work, Khushwant had a wry sense of humor and was a charming conversationalist. He would get up early every morning and work all day on any one of his many projects. He believed in being active in Delhi's society, and suggested I do a radio broadcast about the differences between Indian classical dance and Western classical ballet. He knew of my interest in both dance forms, and since I was the only woman in this Western community studying Indian dance, he thought that sharing my impressions by radio would go over well with the international and local public. He would say to me, "Enough of this gadding about...you must do something. Why not prepare a program about Western classical ballet?"

Khushwant was very persuasive. Whenever we met, he would urge me to develop this radio program—and I finally agreed to do so.

Motivated by Khushwant, and inspired by Mahatma Gandhi's wise adage, "Everything that happens to you is your teacher, the secret is to sit at the feet of your own life and be taught by it," I decided it was time to give some purpose to my life in India, and re-entered the world of radio communications. Giving up many of my social activities, I settled down to write a script about ballet, which I then delivered to the English-speaking "All India Radio" audience. Response from listeners was so positive, I also translated it into French for the francophone listeners. Though my French wasn't perfect, it, too, went over well. My previous experience with radio in New York proved to have been a good foundation for these programs, as I was already

My good friend, author – journalist Khushwant Singh

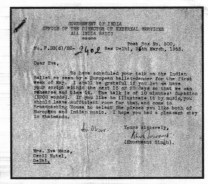

Confirmation of my English radio program for All India's *Of Persons, Places and Things* (center), and Singh's request for a script and rehearsal time (bottom)

59

My *Impressions of Indian Dancing* program
in the "All India Radio" journal

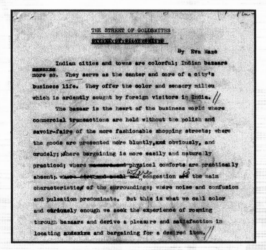

The *Street of Goldsmiths* script for
"All India Radio"

familiar with how to pace my words carefully for radio, and where to include musical excerpts into the dialogue.

In the program, I discussed the history of classical ballet and how it began in the French and Italian courts. Contrary to what many people believe, ballet didn't start in Russia. Its origins can actually be traced to the late medieval courts of the Medicis in Florence, from where it made its way to the French courts. It was introduced to Russia from France in the late 18th century by a variety of teachers, choreographers, and performers. After providing some background information about ballet, I then delved into the history of Indian dance and its relationship to religion and the Hindu gods.

For several months, I also gave ballet lessons to some of the diplomats' children living at the Cecil Hotel, but soon realized that I didn't have the patience that is required for teaching ballet to small children. During that time, my personal life also took a complicated turn when I became involved romantically with a diplomat from one of the Scandinavian countries. I was a young, married mother who was also very romantic, and I guess I fell under the spell of the exotic Indian atmosphere around me. Whether it was the continuous attention of servants waiting on you hand and foot, the intense smells and sounds of New Delhi, the hypnotic

Indian dance rhythms that were forever churning in my head or the romantic Indian fables I loved to read, I ended up casting convention aside and fell in love with a very handsome, sophisticated, older married man. Our feelings for one another were mutual, and though this encounter proved to be brief (we remained with our respective married partners, as we both felt our families came first), it remains to this day one of the more pleasant memories of my years in India.

As a result of the success of my radio shows, I was asked to contribute others. I began commenting on daily life in New Delhi from the perspective of a foreigner. Among the more interesting programs I hosted was one about the silver and gold artisans of Dariba Kalan Street in New Delhi I called "The Street of Goldsmiths." The artists came from generations of families who had designed and created exquisite works of silver and gold. Ornamentation was very important to both women and men in India then, and continues to be a symbol of economic status today, particularly during marriage ceremonies. These beautiful shops filled with glittering gold and silver chains, jewels, tea sets, scent boxes, and carved picture frames stood in sharp contrast to the dirty roads and smelly cows nearby, but this was part of life in the capital and I learned to accept it. Since very few people spoke English at the time (Hindi and its dialects were the most prevalent), I always brought a translator along.

My visit to Nepal had inspired me to visit other Asian countries, so I also decided to take a week's trip to Angkor Wat and Cambodia's capital, Phnom Penh, not knowing whether I would ever have another chance to explore its famous temples. I also needed to be alone for a while to reflect on everything that had happened to me up to that moment.

Angkor Wat – along with other temples dedicated to many of the Hindu gods, especially Vishnu – is considered to be one of the largest religious monuments in the world. Built in the 12th century during the ancient Khmer Empire, and originally connected to Hinduism, Angkor Wat became later known as a Buddhist site. No amount of previous knowledge could have prepared me for the awe I felt upon seeing these amazing sculptures created hundreds of years ago. Many of the figures carved into the walls of the buildings represented "devatas" or divine beings. While made of stone, they seemed to come alive, and their poses reminded me of the movements I was studying in my Indian dance classes. In Phnom Penh I walked around the city by myself for a few days, sightseeing and shopping. The countless displays of beautiful silks, other fabrics, and precious objects were hard to resist.

Dancing Apsara female deities, symbols of
the arts and fertility, carved into the temple
walls of Angkor Wat, Cambodia

Unlike my experiences in Nepal, I had
no connections to the royal court of Cambodia
and knew little about the Khmer Empire. The
country had recently gained independence
from France, and Prince Norodom Sihanouk
occupied the throne. This was the mid-1950s,
before the devastation that occurred during the
Viet Nam War.

My short holiday over, I returned to New
Delhi and prepared for another trip to New York
with Stephanie. I would go back to New York
every year, and make a point to see my good
friends at the ballet studio in Steinway Hall –
as well as be with my mother whom I missed,
and was able to see only sporadically because of
the long distances apart from one-another. My
father had died in 1950, and the only means of
communication across the world then were by
mail and telephone.

On this particular occasion, Ludmilla
Schollar – my former ballet instructor – told me
that one of her students, Marina Svetlova, then
prima ballerina with the Metropolitan Opera
Ballet – was appearing with the London Festival
Ballet as a guest.

It felt good to see Madame Schollar
again and, over lunch at the Russian Tea Room
– her favorite restaurant just on the other side
of 57th Street – she told me emphatically in her
inimitable fashion, "My dear Eva, since you are

going through London on your way back to New Delhi, it's nothing for you to stop and speak to Marina. She and two of her friends are interested in forming a small touring group. Listen – these two friends are Anton Dolin and John Gilpin, and I happen to know they've got this idea of going to Ceylon (now Sri Lanka) for a vacation and that's near you in India. Why don't you think about doing something with them? You know, you would be wonderful. Tell me you'll talk to Marina. I'll give you her number."

"Do you mean that I should organize a tour?"

"Why not?"

"Do I have a choice?" I asked, smiling.

The answer, of course, was "no." You could not refuse Madame Schollar anything. We had become dear friends since that very first day when I cautiously stood at the door of her studio, waiting to talk to her. Also, since I had my three-year-old daughter, Stephanie, with me on this trip, I was hoping Madame Schollar would treat her to one of her classes – and perhaps inspire a little girl to become a future ballerina.

Simply put, my career as an impresario began with this friendly request. Up until that moment, I had never considered the profession of impresario (a.k.a. producer, manager of performing artists, touring manager, booking agent, etc.) – and a female one at that. Nor did I ever dream of perhaps following some day in the footsteps of the most famous Russian-born American impresario of the day, Sol Hurok. For more than 50 years under "S. Hurok Presents," this illustrious manager of top talent in the performing arts would represent and tour renowned artists, including Isadora Duncan, Margot Fonteyn, Van Cliburn, Andrés Segovia, Arthur Rubinstein, Marian Anderson, Michel Fokine, and Isaac Stern, among many others. In the 1920s and 1930s, Hurok became known for bringing Russian ballerina Anna Pavlova to the United States, and for touring the Ballets Russes de Monte Carlo in America (following Diaghilev's earlier successful Ballets Russes tours there). Hurok was also the first to have introduced ballet to India with Pavlova in the 1920s, but classical ballet had not been presented in that country since then.

Madame Schollar was convinced that I could – and should – bring Marina and her friends to India. By the time I reached London, she had already contacted Marina, who was then guesting for the London Festival Ballet with Dolin and Gilpin. Agreeing to meet with me, Marina mentioned the trio was very enthusiastic about doing a ballet tour in India, but that they would

Anna Pavlova, after her
1922 debut in India

Legendary impresario Sol Hurok in the 1960s,
who was a source of inspiration for me

Serge Diaghilev, who
brought ballet to India

only do so if they could stop in Ceylon for a short holiday. I concurred with her request, but also told her that a final commitment on my part would depend entirely on receiving financial backing there.

Back in New Delhi, I threw myself into this new adventure, and began making contacts and arrangements for an actual tour. The initial feedback was amazing. Both local citizens and members of the foreign community responded enthusiastically with names and suggestions – as well as financial support – and I could hardly believe that I was actually about to launch a ballet tour in India, with stars from the Metropolitan Opera Ballet and the London Festival, no less! Instinctively, I also realized that, if successful, this might also be the auspicious beginning of a new career for me, one that very few women, if any, had embarked on at the time.

Knowing that the concert-going public in India tended to be somewhat conservative, and I needed to give the tour respectability, I first asked for the support of government officials and contacted Maharani Rahjkumari Amrit Kaur, India's Minister of Health. The minister graciously agreed to lend her name as a patron – which, in turn, became an important acknowledgement

With (l to r) Tikki Oberoi, his brother Biki Oberoi, who financed my
first ballet tour in India, and Amitava Nandi

With Svetlova and pianist Haig (bottom),
and (l to r) Dolin and Gilpin (top)

of this new venture. I was then introduced to Bikki Oberoi of the well-known Oberoi family, who owned a number of hotels in India, as well as a travel agency. He, in turn, decided to back the entire tour, with part of the proceeds from the performances going to the Indian Council for Child Welfare, of which Maharani Amrit Kaur was president. The Council had been established in 1948 to help children who had been uprooted by the partition and were victims of poverty, neglect, and exploitation, among other calamities.

Bikki and I agreed on a per diem for the dancers, and on having their hotel and airfares – including their short stay in Ceylon – covered. I personally chose not to receive a salary, but did end up with a small profit of about one thousand dollars from the ticket sales when the tour was finished. With these initial earnings as an impresario, I bought myself a magnificent sitar that still stands in my living-room today.

We – Marina Svetlova, Anton Dolin, John Gilpin, their pianist Theodor Haig, and I – opened in Bombay (now Mumbai) at the Excelsior Theatre, the same theater where the legendary ballerina, Anna Pavlova, had danced on her visit to India in the 1920s. Shrimati Ratan Kumar

BALLET

MARINA SVETLOVA

ANTON DOLIN

JOHN GILPIN

WITH

THEODOR HAIG
CONCERT PIANIST

PRESENTED BY EVA MAZE

INDIA TOUR 1953

1953 *Ballet Concert Series* program cover featuring prima ballerina Marina Svetlova

(R.K.) Nehru, cousin of Jawaharlal Nehru, who was Secretary General of the Indian Ministry of Foreign Affairs, formally inaugurated the "Ballet Concert Series." The newspaper publicity we received was astounding. Bringing western classical ballet to India was then an unusual concept, and it was a challenge to open in Bombay, which was home primarily to the Indian movie industry. Then entering its Golden Age, the city was churning out dozens of serious theme-based movies each year about life in India (*Pyaasa, Mother India…*) that went on to win many foreign awards. It was also producing lighter romantic films intended for a mass audience that featured imaginative dance sequences based on classical Indian dance styles and ancient myths, which would eventually lead to the more modern and very popular "Bollywood" films in the late 1990s. Classical ballet was clearly something different.

All of us were pleasantly surprised. Whether it was the Indian public's curiosity about classical ballet, the ramped-up newspaper and radio publicity, or just a novelty to cultural life in India, we ended up with a full house on opening night. Representatives from the film industry, upper class Brahmin couples, and Parsis (families of Zoroastrian-Iranian descent whose ancestors settled in the Bombay area in the 10th century after fleeing the Muslims) were among those who attended that night – and every night thereafter.

October 1953 reception with the Pakistani Commissioner to India (center), hosted by Delhi Little Theatre in our apartment

Diplomat Shrimati R. K. Nehru (second from right) opens the *Ballet Concert Series* in New Delhi

In Bombay, with (l to r) Theodor Haig, Marina Svetlova, Anton Dolin, and John Gilpin

On the second day, however, we ran into some serious problems. Theodore Haig, our pianist and Marina Svetlova's friend, informed me that he could no longer play with his right hand because of an infected finger. He was afraid that the continuous pounding of the piano keys would cause permanent damage to his hand, and that this would end his career. His finger had apparently been caught in the hinge of his car door in London before the trip, had become infected, and had taken a turn for the worse. He hadn't told me anything about this prior to my hiring him and had been trying to manage as best he could with his other fingers. No classical pianist was available for another six concerts, and if there were no pianist, there would, of course, be no dancing. Each day, we anxiously wondered whether the curtain would go up…. I, along with the dancers, was there, crossing my fingers at the beginning of each performance.

Somehow, we made it through Bombay and headed for New Delhi with the injured pianist. The dancers knew there would be another pianist waiting for us in Calcutta, (now Kolkata), but that he would only be available after our next performance in New Delhi.

Then, much to my chagrin, another issue surfaced upon our arrival in Delhi: The concert hall where we were scheduled to perform had no piano (bad luck seemed to follow us everywhere!), and we absolutely had to find a piano to continue the tour…. This time, my husband and a friend of his came to our rescue.

Oscar was an avid tennis player who often played matches with Captain Srinavasan, bodyguard of President Rajendra Prasad of India, at the Gymkana Tennis Club of New Delhi. The club was home to the best Indian players at that time, Narendra Nath and Naresh Kumar. Eager to help us, Captain Srinavasan proceeded to have President Prasad's personal grand piano picked up at his palace residence and transported by wooden cart pulled by bullocks to our concert hall – and it thankfully arrived in time for our show.

Then there were further complications…

One of the three dancers, Anton Dolin, was now in his late 40s and showing signs of age. He, however, was important to the tour. People knew his name and he was therefore a big draw. He had been the dance partner of Alicia Markova, one of Britain's finest prima ballerinas. The international members of the audience, who were familiar with classical ballet would recognize the names of both Markova and Dolin and thus be more inclined to buy tickets to this event. I had to make a decision on how to present him without making his age obvious.

The Indian Woman's
Trend
Editor: FRENE TALYARKHAN
VOLUME 1. NO. 17   SEPTEMBER 26, 1953

4 AS.

EVA MAZE; AN IMPRESARIO IS BORN

"OPERATION BALLET"

"PLEASE put the word 'impresario' in quotes ... you know I am only a novice!" explained a smiling, dark-haired young woman as she spoke to a group of Bombay newspapermen. But this novice has little cause to worry. When nearly next month renowned ballet dancers Marina Svetlova, Anton Dolin and John Gilpin come to India, Eva Maze will enjoy the distinction of becoming one of the world's few women impresarios.

The Rajmata-born, American-naturalised wife of one of Pan-Am's chiefs in New Delhi, Mrs. Maze decided a year ago that she could no longer follow the usual pattern of a foreigner's life in India. Keeping house, issuing parties and reading books was fun but she wanted to return to her one-time career, the Ballet. Her training began at the age of four in her own country, continued in the USA under some of the best known maestros. Came college, a brief but interesting spell of varied jobs (Eva speaks seven languages), later, marriage.

Armed with little knowledge of business, but blessed with abundant energy and enthusiasm, impresario Maze has planned the tour of the three dancers with the aid of an enterprising Indian backer. In Bombay she will present her group in association with Trend and the Bombay Municipal Singers' Organisation.

BALLET TROUPE IN DELHI

OCTOBER 7, 1953 (3)

WESTERN ART TO BE ON DISPLAY

Four Performances Planned

Fresh from a blazing triumph at Bombay's Excelsior, the four-member team from London's Festival Ballet arrived in New Delhi on Tuesday.

The troupe consists of Marina Svetlova, Anton Dolin, John Gilpin and Theodor Haig. They will give four performances in the capital on Wednesday, Thursday and Friday at the National Physical Laboratory.

For the opening and the last night, both beginning at 9-30 p.m., the programme will include Act I of the Swan Lack Ballet (Tchaikovsky), featuring all the three artistes. John Gilpin will render "Spiritual" (Don Gillis), Anton Dolin the hymn to the sun (Rimskay-Korsekov) and The Puppet (Stravisky) and Marina Svetlova the dance of the Elfs (Rimsky-Korsekov). Besides, with Dolin, Svetlova will play the Pas de Deux from "Don Quixote" (Minkus) and with Gilpin the Blue Danube (Straus) and Pas de Deux from Act II of the "Nut Cracker" ballet (Techaikovsky).

TWO SHOWS

On Thursday, at 5-30 p.m. and again at 9-30 p.m., the programme will begin with Suite de Danses (Chopin) with all three, followed by Variation "Vestris" (Rossini) by John Gilpin, Diana, the Huntress (Liszt) by Svetlova; Harlequinade (Drigo) by Svetlova and Gilpin, Italian Suite (Cimarosa) by Svetlova and Dolin; two preludes (Greshwin) by Gilpin, the Tragedy of Marguerite (Schuman) by Marina, The Black Swan from The Swan Svetlova, and Pas de Deux Lake (Tchaikovski) by Svetlova and Gilpin.

Theodore Haig will render on the first and last nights Schuman's Arabesk Opus 18, and Chopin's Ballade in G. Minor, Opus 23, and on Thursday a Chopin-Liszt Polish Song and Rachmaninov's Prelude Opus 5, No. 2; Rondo Capriccioso, Opus 14 (Mindelssohn) and Chopin's Nocturne and Ballade in a Fiat Opus 47.

The four-member troupe from London's Festival Ballet on arrival in Delhi on Tuesday. The prima ballerina, Marina Svetlova, is second from the left. The tour has been organised by Mrs. Eva Maze (extreme left).

DISORDER AT POLLING BOOTH ALLEGED

Delhi Election Petition

Arguments began on Tuesday before the Delhi State Election Tribunal in the election petition filed by Bawa Bachitter Singh challenging the election of Mr. G. L. Salwan to the Delhi State Assembly from the Jhandewalan constituency.

Counsel for the petitioner argued that there was no dispute regarding the validity of the acceptance of the nomination papers of the petitioner. He said although the duly nominated candidates had been implanted as respondents, they had not filed any written statement.

Mr. Parshotam Lal, a member

NO MASS AKALI RESIGNATIONS

Mr. B. Singh's Claim Denied By Party

By A Staff Reporter

Sardar Autar Singh and Sardar Richhpal Singh, President and General Secretary of the Delhi State branch of the Akali Dal, have repudiated Sardar Balwant Singh's claim that nearly 1,000 Akalis had resigned from the Dal as a protest against its "reactionary policies."

According to the Akali Dal leaders, only eight resignations had been received so far. Of them, two members had indicated their desire to withdraw their resignations.

This is the first time, since Pavlova's visit a quarter of a century ago, that Western classical ballet dancers are performing in India. The purpose of the tour, according to Eva Maze, its organiser, is to bring the real Western ballet before Indian audiences who, she feels, get only an "ersatz" version of the art in the films.

Time of India Bombay
Sept 20, 1953

ES OF INDIA

BALLET DANCERS FROM EUROPE TO TOUR INDIA

Bombay, Oct 34th   Exclusive Tour

By A Staff Reporter

A PARTY of famous Western classical ballet dancers will tour India shortly to present for the first time since the celebrated Anna Pavlova a serious of performances in this country.

The ballet will consist of Marina Svetlova, prima ballerina, Anton Dolin, art director and premier danseur, John Gilpin, premier danseur, and Theodor Haig, concert pianist.

The group is scheduled to arrive in Bombay early in the first week of October and is expected to appear the Regarding Vishnu Bhavan on October 3, 5 and 6.

After the Bombay session, the dancers will proceed to Delhi where they will take the floor at the National Physical Laboratory hall on the evenings of October 7, 8 and 9. They will conclude their season in Calcutta where they will put on the boards a series of ballets from October 11 to 15.

Mrs. Eva Maze, herself a noted dancer, who is the organiser of the above ballet concerts, stated in Bombay on Saturday that the purpose of bringing out such a well-known dancers to India was to strengthen cultural bonds between this country and the West, besides giving an opportunity to Indians to witness classical western dancing. She said she was aware of the fact that Lovers of Art in India had always displayed a keen interest in ballet danc-

ing and the artistes who were to tour this country were pleased to exhibit their talents to the Indian audience. They were equally desirous of improving cultural relations and exchanging further knowledge of the respective dance forms of India and the West.

NOTED ARTISTES

Mrs. Maze hoped that the first appearance of outstanding dancers since Pavlova would be a great draw. The artistes were at present with London's Festival Ballet, performing at the Royal Festival Hall, and were internationally famous for many years. Marina Svetlova was guest ballerina with the Festival Ballet and had appeared earlier this year in various centres with Yehudi Menuhin and Segovia participating in some of the performances.

Anton Dolin holds a unique place in the history of English ballet. John Gilpin has been one of the leading dancers since the Festival Ballet was started. Though only 23 years he has been described as one of the most graceful male dancers.

Mrs. Maze, the initiator of the venture and the Impresaria for the group during its Indian tour, has had a remarkable dancing career. She has toured extensively in the U.S. and more recently was featured in the B.B.C. television programme. Since taking up residence in Delhi some time ago, she has been evincing keen interest in Indian dancing.

Mrs. Eva Maze

NEW DELHI NOTEBOOK

OCTOBER 4, 1953 (13)

For Balletomanes

THERE is great news for lovers of the ballet. Three top-ranking dancers, members of the

Royal Festival Ballet, London, are coming to show India Western ballet. The last time we saw classical Western ballet here, not on the cinema screen, was when Anna Pavlova came; before that the only name which springs to my mind is that of the notorious Lola Montez!

The artistic director and the premier dancer of the troupe is the famed Anton Dolin (alias Patrick Healey-Kay of Sussex) whom the immortal Diaghileff picked out as one of his dancers, and who partnered such great ballerinas as Karsavina, Nemchinova, Nijinska and Markova. From 1931 to 1935 Dolin was principal dancer at the Vic-Wells Ballet. Two years ago he founded the Festival Ballet, of which he is still Artistic Director.

The prima ballerina is the Russian-born Marina Svetlova who has worked with Serge Lifar and Diaghileff, and has toured half the earth. For several years she has danced in the USA where she was prima ballerina of the Metropolitan Opera—a position that was vacant for a decade. For some time now she has been guest ballerina of Dolin's Festival Ballet.

Dolin himself, though getting on in years, is still a nimble and active dancer. He is bringing with him one of England's most promising young dancers, John Gilpin, who is 23 and has been the premier danseur of the Festival Ballet under Dolin. When I saw him a year or so ago, I found him talented, graceful and with an absolutely correct classical technique.

The well-known American concert pianist, Mr. Theoor Haig is going to accompany the dancers, and also give a recital.

The provisional dates for Delhi are October 5, 6 and 7, with a matinee on October 7; before that they may perform in Bombay and dates have also been fixed for Calcutta at the New Empire. Here they will give their shows at the National Physical Laboratory, and the programme will include excerpts from such famous classical ballets as "Swan Lake", "Giselle" and "Les Sylphides".

Prices will be reasonable, for this is a goodwill visit to a country famous for her own classical dancing.

Behind this important art event modestly stands an American ballet dancer, Mrs Eva Maze, who has arranged the visit entirely single-handed, from the first letter to Anton Dolin to the printing of the posters and tickets. Mrs Maze has been living in India for the last few years after a career as a ballet dancer in the United States and in England. Devoted to her art with a single-minded sincerity and fervour, she gave a talk last spring to the Delhi Critics' Circles which made a deep impression on her audience. She has been studying Bharata Natya since coming to India

Not only has she obtained this fine troupe of dancers but also the financial backing that makes such a goodwill visit possible. This is no small matter, as those who have sympathetically watched the struggles of the Delhi Music Society—and their failures—know only too well.

Ballet tour reviews by the
Indian press

We both decided it was best to have him appear in a simpler role on stage, and as little as possible. So he was given one dance – a piano piece called *Hymn to the Sun*, by Rimsky-Korsakov – with a part that was more mime than dance, which he was happy to do.

In the meantime, I was in my fourth month of pregnancy with my second daughter, Lauri. Dolin, who had a dry sense of humor, made a point of saying that this was the first time he had been "represented by a pregnant impresario" – which amused everyone, including me.

Prima Ballerina Marina Svetlova and the young, handsome John Gilpin received huge accolades from both the critics and audiences. Our performances were among the highlights of the social season in all three cities. In New Delhi, we had the honor of having the entire diplomatic community in attendance, as well as Minister Jawaharlal Nehru's sister, Vijaya Lakshmi Pandit, who later became the first woman to serve as president of the United Nations General Assembly. Top government officials were also present at the event, including President Rajendra Prasad, India's first president. An amazing man in his own right, he had fought alongside Mahatma Gandhi through several Satyagrahas (non-violent protests) for India's independence from the British in 1947.

Through the grapevine, the story of the injured pianist reached another diplomat, the French cultural attaché to India. Aware of our predicament, he graciously arranged for a pianist to come from Pondicherry – an eastern seaside town on the Bay of Bengal in India – to Calcutta and replace the pianist with the injured finger. Shortly before leaving for their final shows in Calcutta, the dancers, however, balked at performing further, concerned about working with a new pianist. So, for the first time in my very young career as a manager, I summoned my courage and offered them an ultimatum: They would either work with this new musician or immediately fly back to London without visiting Ceylon (I still had their tickets). Thankfully, they relented and we continued on with the performances. And I, with all of my limited six months' experience as an impresario, was beginning to grasp just how complicated this business could be. I would need to learn how and when to assert myself; how to deal with different types of personalities and egos; how to be organized and anticipate potential last-minute problems; how to calmly make decisions without wearing myself down in the face of emergencies; and how to negotiate wisely. My college degree in psychology would certainly come in handy, as I expected there would be many tough situations ahead if I continued down this career path.

The day after the last Delhi performance, the foursome took the plane to Calcutta and finished the tour, as per their contract. We ended up by using both pianists, one playing with his right hand, the other, with his left, and the dancers rehearsed with them for four hours straight. The tour ended on a high note, and after the final six shows in Calcutta, I put them all on a plane, wished them a wonderful vacation, and took a deep breath. I also told myself I would never tour with another dancer again, and that, if ever one were needed, it would just have to be me. Between my pregnancy and the tension caused by the tour, I was completely exhausted. To recover, I went to the mountains of Darjeeling, and prepared for the birth of my baby.

My first daughter, Stephanie, had been delivered at Doctor's Hospital in New York City, and since I wanted both children to be born in the United States, I returned to New York for the birth of my second child, Lauri. But this time, I was cutting it close. The Pan Am stewardess took one look at me as I boarded the flight and panicked. She quickly consulted a baby delivery manual and two hours into the flight, I began to have contractions. The flight attendants started prepping for a possible delivery and were certain the baby would be born on the plane. Yet nature took its own course (it was false labor), and it actually took Lauri another two days before announcing herself to the world at Doctor's Hospital.

After visiting my mother in New York, I returned to New Delhi a week later only to learn that, again, we were on our way to a new assignment. It was 1954, and Oscar was being transferred to another city – this time back to Europe to Frankfurt/Main, Germany. We would remain there for 12 years and it would become one of the most prolific periods of my life.

At the age of 32, I was slowly coming into my own: I had graduated from a good college; spoke a number of languages; had a succinct understanding of classical ballet and other dance forms; had lived in a variety of foreign cultures; had performed on stage; and had seen many stage performances in London and New York. I had also successfully tried my hand at a new career which, though filled with obstacles, was beginning to fascinate me. I was intrigued by the process and liked the feeling of satisfaction it gave me. So after my delivery – and some time off with my new baby and family – I returned to what had motivated me in the first place: my passion for ballet. And despite my vow of never touring with dancers again, I decided to follow my instincts and my heart, and throw myself seriously into my new profession of choice – that of impresario. Starting with the world of dance, my goals became clear: I would search for unique talent, manage an international array of artists of quality from all over the world, and introduce these artists and their talent to new audiences around the world.

I also was aware that I was entering uncharted territory as a woman, and would probably be one of the first female impresarios to do so. It wasn't going to be easy, and I would be operating in a man's world at a time when – at least in the United States – a woman's place was at home, preparing meals for her husband and taking care of her children. This was, after all, the 1950s, and women/mothers were not supposed to have professional careers, or be fielding phone calls all day long from an office at home, or negotiating contracts and ticket sales, or be traveling on the road with temperamental artists. But I felt that if, in my first venture as an impresario, I was able to organize and manage such a difficult tour in a challenging country like India, I would surely be able to handle most of the professional – and personal – obstacles that lay ahead. I also was convinced that, not only could I make a living at pursuing this fascinating profession, I could actually become successful at it.

Inspired by Sol Hurok and knowing we would be living in Frankfurt for at least four years, I then decided to form my own company under Eva Maze Presents/ International Artists Productions. It would reflect my own vision of the world of dance, music, and theater, and oversee a variety of theatrical productions dear to my heart. I also knew that Oscar, who had always been supportive of my interests and activities, would be by my side.

Post-tour portrait before
leaving for Frankfurt, Germany

The American WEEKEND Entertainment Guide — Jan 1, (54)

Housewife Becomes An Impressario

Take a little chunk of your husband's capital, add a bit of your own imagination, spice it up with many hours of hard work—and you'll become a businesswoman.

It's just happened in Frankfurt, Germany. The energetic young woman involved is Mrs. Eva Maze, American wife of an airline executive, who's become an impressario.

Mrs. Maze, an active member of the Frankfurt International Women's Club, is presenting a 22-year-old classic Spanish dancer in her first tour of Germany—and she's hoping that many other Americans will become interested in her venture and attend the dance concerts.

A former ballet dancer herself, Mrs. Maze previously got briefly into the impressario business when she and her family were living in India. She was responsible for bringing the London Festival Ballet dancers on a tour of India. She's now starting as an impressario in Germany.

The dancer first being presented is Tere Amoros, who appeared in the United States last year in a recital at Carnegie Hall and has since had several top appearances in Europe.

Daughter of a Spanish bullfighter, she brings the fire and excitement of this bloodthirsty sport to the dance stage. She'll dance to the music of Spain's top composers, Granados, De Falla and Albeniz, in her German tour. Her dances range from the classic Spanish numbers to the spirited flamencos and numbers based on the rich folklore of her native land.

Tere Amoros makes her first German appearance January 5 at the Hessiches Staatstheater in Wiesbaden. She will subsequently dance at Bad Nauheim on January 9, Frankfurt's Kleines Haus January 17 and Karlsruhe's Badisches Staatstheater January 18.

★ ★ ★

Young American housewife Eva Maze first got a taste of show business when she presented a ballet in India.

5. Frankfurt

We arrived in Frankfurt/Main, Germany, in 1954, and my company, International Artists Productions, was established soon thereafter. Nine years had passed since the end of World War II, and Frankfurt was still recovering from the damage caused by Allied bombs. A number of neighborhoods were being rebuilt, including the downtown area of the city.

The Potsdam Agreement of 1945 had sealed the fate of Germany as a divided country by the three Allies of World War II: Britain's Prime Minister Clement Attlee, who had replaced Winston Churchill in the 1945 British elections; President of the United States, Harry S. Truman, newly appointed after Roosevelt's death in 1945; and Joseph Stalin, who had become General Secretary of the Union of Soviet Socialist Republics. This division was to last more than 40 years, until the fall of the Berlin Wall in 1989.

In the immediate years following the war, Germany lay in rubble, with its population vastly displaced. As with London, food was tightly rationed until 1948 and reconstruction dominated the scene. However, while London was tagged as a "hardship" post for Pan Am in the late

Frankfurt/Main postwar downtown reconstruction (left), and
Hauptwache district in the center of the city (right), early 1950s

1940s, a feeling of normalcy had already settled into Frankfurt in the early 1950s with the help of the Marshall Plan under Presidents Truman and Eisenhower, and this city was viewed as a normal assignment. Stores were stocked with a wide variety of food and even some luxury items; there was no shortage of electricity, water, or coal; trolleys and trains ran on time; and people, once again, resumed one of their favorite pastimes: going to the theater.

Nevertheless, Germany in 1954 was – both physically and emotionally – still in a state of disarray and shock, as it grappled with its defeat, division, and understanding of what had actually transpired under the Nazis. While the Germans were confronted daily by the devastation of their country and the horrors inflicted under Hitler, Nazi sentiment continued to lurk in the shadows of some circles, and we, as a family, never spoke about our Jewish heritage. And though parts of the city had been revitalized with modern buildings and infrastructure, a number of neighborhoods still remained dilapidated or empty.

Knowing the organized nature of the Germans, I, however, was certain that Frankfurt – along with other German cities destroyed by the Allies – would become the thriving centers they once were. Prior to and during the war, Frankfurt/Main had been known as the financial center of Germany, and the city would eventually return to its pre-war status. Today, it serves as one of the most important commercial centers in the world.

The bombed-out Alte Oper/ Old Frankfurt Opera House ruin (left),
and our first apartment building on Staufenstrasse (right)

As neighborhoods and communities slowly came back to life, one of the many landmarks of the city that still remained in ruins was the once famous Old Frankfurt Opera House, the "Alte Oper." Built in 1880 under Kaiser Wilhelm I, and bombed in 1944, it was a shell of its former self. Charred and hollow, it was a grim reminder of the effects of the war, and the remains of its Renaissance-style facade became known as "Germany's most beautiful ruin." The opera house would not be rebuilt until 1981, with funds organized by a citizens' campaign initiative. In the meantime, all opera and theatrical productions – from the 1950s through the 1970s – were held nearby at the New Frankfurt Opera and Theater (Neue Frankfurter Oper und Schauspielhaus), under the Frankfurt/Main city-run "Städtische Bühnen" (Municipal Theaters of Frankfurt/Main).

We first settled into a modern three-bedroom apartment on Staufenstrasse not far from the Old Opera House, near a small park and playground where my children could play, then moved to a larger flat on Schumanstrasse, close to the famous Palmengarten botanical gardens, in an area called the West Ende (West End).

Oscar shuttled back and forth to work at Frankfurt Airport every day. Pan Am was expanding rapidly in the 1950s, adding new fleets of planes and routes to its system. The company's aircraft in those days included the famous Stratocruiser, known for its double-deck fuselage. The lower-deck, featuring a lounge with bar and seats for people to socialize, led, by circular stairs, to an upper deck, replete with sleeping berths above the passenger seats, in the area now used for modern-day roller bags. Similar to old overnight trains, the berths allowed people the privacy of sleeping behind pulled curtains. This elegant airplane – and my favorite at the time – is where I almost gave birth to my younger daughter, Lauri, on my way from New Delhi to New York.

Traveling by air in the mid-fifties took time. In 1958, for example, a trip from Los Angeles to Tokyo by Stratocruiser lasted more than 30 hours. Eventually deemed too costly, this majestic plane would be replaced by a variety of other aircraft: first, the more efficient Lockheed Constellation (competing with TWA's extensive and expensive fleet), and Douglas DC 6s and 7s propeller aircraft series, which cut flying time across the Atlantic (a non-stop flight from Idlewild / Kennedy Airport in New York to London took close to 11 hours); then, the wide-body DC 8s, seating six passengers across each aisle and Boeing 707s, which ushered in the age of jetliners in 1958, enabling non-stop transatlantic travel; and finally the jumbo jet 747s, which became the "queens" of the fleet. From its initial South American routes, Pan Am expanded into European countries beyond Britain and Ireland – and into Asia, Africa, and the Middle-East.

Pan Am Stratocruiser taxiing into Idlewild (later Kennedy)
Airport, Queens, New York, 1951

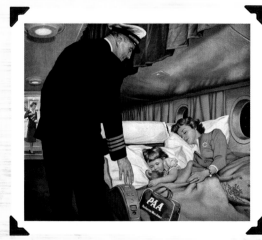

Vintage illustration of a mother and child
sleeping aboard a Pan Am Stratocruiser

Frankfurt would become one of Pan Am's most important hubs, both for international travel and within Germany itself through the Internal German Service (IGS), where my husband worked. Established in accordance with post-war agreements with the Soviets, pilots had to follow specific flight paths and air corridors, in and out of Berlin. Lufthansa, Germany's national airline, was forbidden from flying to and from the divided city for as long as the Soviet Union controlled East Germany, and the IGS developed into a very profitable division for the airline.

As for me, I went back to studying ballet. My London friends had suggested I contact a ballet mistress by the name of Tatiana Gsovsky, who was director of both the Frankfurt and Berlin Operas in Germany, as well as a well-known choreographer, and she allowed me to take classes with the Frankfurt Ballet. A slender woman in her late seventies with peppered black and white hair, she was meticulous, methodical, demanding, and stern, very much in keeping with the Russian style of ballet teaching. As a choreographer, she had dominated the dance scene in Germany for more than 20 years with ballet stagings of such works as Sergei Prokofiev's *Romeo and Juliet* and Kurt Weill's *Seven Deadly Sins*.

When we first met, she was preparing the ballet, *Sleeping Beauty* with music by Peter Ilyich Tchaikovsky, and after coaching me for several months, asked me to step in for a dancer, who

1950s Pan Am Lockheed Constellation aircraft illustration

Early 1960s jet-powered Pan Am 707 in flight

Dancing as the Queen Mother (center) in Frankfurt Ballet's
production of *Sleeping Beauty*

Around the Pas-de-Deux
German television program
announcement

was leaving the production to get married. It was a small character dance part that involved little more than pantomime and a mazurka (a polka-like dance of Polish origin). I was to play the role of the queen, mother of Princess Aurora, in the wedding scene of the third act. I accepted – but only for ten performances. My career was now moving in a different direction, and I didn't wish to become known as someone who was eager to be on stage. I did, however, want to complete my task in a professional manner – and had a lot of fun doing so in the process.

During one of the evening performances, an amusing incident occurred when my dance partner, the ballet instructor of the Frankfurt Ballet at that time, Michael Piel – then in his fifties and playing the role of the king – forgot to take his glasses off before appearing on stage for this dance. Of course, this made a number of us laugh, and, in a whisper, I quickly reminded him of his oversight (the glasses were not part of the act, and he promptly threw them to a stagehand in the wings). The evening performances were attended by family and friends, much to the delight of my children (we were amused when my older daughter, Stephanie, who had begun taking ballet, thought I was a better queen than the dancer who would later take over from me).

During this time, I also became involved with local German television – the Hessische Rundfunk – and was asked to produce a program for the station about ballet movements and language. Since much of ballet evolved in the courts of Louis XIV of France, most of its classical steps have French names. It was to be a narrated 45-minute show called "Rund um den Pas-de-Deux" (Around the Pas-de-Deux). As producer, this was my first introduction to television, which, in those days, was still broadcast in black and white. The idea was to demonstrate and talk about various ballet steps. I had become friends with the two leading soloists of the Frankfurt Opera Ballet, Maria Fris and Rainer Köchermann, who agreed to participate in the program by introducing and discussing different moves that are part of the ballet repertoire, such as the "Grand Jeté" and the "Pas-de-Deux." Though both did a terrific job, I remember Maria as being somewhat uncomfortable in front of the camera. She was a wonderful dancer, but she was also self-conscious about the large calves of her legs, especially when the camera focused on the lower part of her body.

This extremely difficult and all-consuming art form that is known as ballet is very image-conscious. It requires tremendous physical (and emotional) effort to excel in it, and the process for being admitted into a company is rigorous and competitive. Dancers must remain limber at all times and, in doing so, are required to take intensive classes on a daily basis. When preparing for a stage production, they often have to rehearse more than eight hours a day. Mastery of poses and jumps – along with complete muscle control and flexibility – are essential. The angle at which a body is viewed in the mirror of a studio, or on stage, is also crucial. This includes how parts of the body, such as calves, thighs or curved in-steps – the area between the toes and the ankle of the foot, which needs to be rounded for maximum effect – have developed.

In the case of the German television production, both Maria and Rainer did a great job, but additional programs were unfortunately cancelled. Several years later, I was saddened to learn that Maria had fallen to her death from a catwalk in the Hamburg Opera House at the age of 29. Whether it was accidental or deliberate was not known, but it was very painful for those who knew her, and a reminder that ballet is a grueling profession that can take a heavy toll on both the body and mind.

Soon after the television program, I became involved in my first ventures as an impresario in Europe, including one that would both become embroiled in the politics of the times, and

First Chamber Dance Quartet performing *Nagare*, set to an 18th century
traditional Japanese song (left), and the evening program (right).

also help launch – in a positive way – my name and company in the burgeoning performing arts community of Germany.

In the late 1950s and 1960s – true to my love for ballet – I first engaged two young companies that were gaining momentum with the American and European public at the time: The First Chamber Dance Quartet from the United States, and Het Nederlands Ballet from Holland.

The First Chamber Dance Quartet was a small dance company of renowned soloists who had performed with leading ballet companies, such as the New York City Ballet, Jerome Robbins' Ballet USA, the American Ballet Theatre, and the Ballets Russes de Monte Carlo. Its founding members – Charles Bennett, William Carter, Lois Bewley, and later Janice Groman – were interested in expanding their artistic vision through ballet, and sought to experiment with innovative choreography, set designs, and costumes. The original company was set up by the four dancers after they had appeared together at the 1960 Pablo Casals Festival of Puerto Rico. A fifth, very talented member – Nadine Revene – was later added to the group as both a dancer and choreographer. Collectively, they began to create highly original works based on classical music (Chopin, Bach, Vivaldi, Boccherini, Schumann, Varèse, Shostakovich), as well as

Japanese folk songs. Known for their personalized "free style" movements, the dancers performed to enthusiastic acclaim by both the media and the public in high schools, colleges, and YMCA auditoriums across the country. I represented them exclusively in West Germany, and took them on a very successful tour to four cities: Frankfurt, Köln, Ludwigshafen, and Hamburg.

A second ballet company making headlines in the late 1950s – that also toured with me through Germany – was Het Nederlands Ballet, under artistic director Sonia Gaskell and the renowned American ballet master, Karel Shook, who later co-founded the Dance Theatre of Harlem. One of the first ballet companies to include an African-American leading soloist, Billy Wilson, Het Nederlands would eventually merge with the Amsterdams Ballet in August 1961 to become the Dutch National Ballet – Holland's official ballet company – which celebrated its 50th anniversary in 2011.

Sonia Gaskell's story is interesting in its own right: Born in Lithuania to Jewish parents, she had studied ballet in Ukraine, left for what was then Palestine to escape Russian anti-Jewish pogroms, and had come to Paris, France, where she danced in nightclubs and cabarets. For a brief time – from 1927 to 1929 –

Frankfurt's Großes Haus
Saturday, April 15, 1961, 22:45 hours.

Het Nederlands Ballet program cover (top) and *Stars and Stripes'* review of Billy Wilson (left) and company in Béjart's *Le Cercle* (top center), Perrot's *Giselle* (top right), and Balanchine's *The Four Temperaments* (bottom)

she also performed with the original Ballets Russes. In Paris, she met her future Dutch husband, and later moved with him to Amsterdam, where she gave clandestine dance classes during the Nazi occupation of Holland. She became the founder of the Het Netherlands Ballet Academy in The Hague, and would also hold the position of artistic director of the Dutch National Ballet from 1961 to 1968. Among the many talents she nurtured as a teacher was a young Audrey Hepburn, who had started out as a ballet dancer before becoming an actress.

Performing Adolphe Adam's classic ballet *Giselle*, Balanchine's *The Four Temperaments*, and a more contemporary work by Maurice Béjart, *The Circle*, the Het Nederlands Ballet received rave reviews from the German press, as well as the *Stars and Stripes* military newspaper on its first tour of eight performances through Germany..

While both ballet companies were on the road, I became involved with a number of other productions in those early years between 1958 and 1963, which often required me to travel, and be away from my family. Because of our flying privileges with Pan Am, my mother, Liza, would come over from New York for months at time to be with us and take care of my children, Stephanie and Lauri. Both she – along with my very supportive husband – made sure that my children's needs were met, that they got to school on time, did their homework, and had a healthy social life. No question in my mind that their support – both personal and financial – was invaluable to me throughout my entire career. Without it, I would have never been able to pursue my dreams or goals. Neither would I have ever been able to engage in the many complicated ventures that lay ahead, including one that would become one of the most challenging projects of my professional life.

After an earlier visit to Paris looking for theatrical talent, I had learned through a French producer friend of mine, George Olivier, about the American musical, *West Side Story* (composed by Leonard Bernstein and choreographed by Jerome Robbins) that had enjoyed considerable success on Broadway. It had also just completed a good run in Paris.

As a young impresario in Europe, I wanted to try something new, and, venturing out of the world of ballet into that of musical theater, made the ambitious decision to bring the show to Germany – and to open with it in Berlin. This required – in those days – an investment of $15,000 a week to cover the per diem salaries and expenses of a cast of 30, hiring of orchestras in every city, prop rentals, and transportation. George Olivier, who had overseen the Paris tour, chose to

Oscar and I welcome my mother, Liza, at Frankfurt Airport,
with our daughters Stephanie (left) and Lauri (center)

become my partner, as well as the road manager for the show. Together, we decided to back the German venture ourselves – each contributing $40,000 to the project. My husband, Oscar, helped me underwrite my half.

The overseas rights were held by a well-known impresario from Israel, Giora Godik. Any impresario or agent wishing to present the musical at specific venues had to sub-contract with him. It was a huge risk – one that made me quite uneasy – but I was swayed by my colleague, George, who was convinced it would be a big hit. Because of the success of *West Side Story* in Paris, I took him at his word and dove in.

What we did not do, however, was sign a good contract. We were relatively new to this game, and I failed to have it reviewed by an attorney. In fact, the contract was so bad that it required a 75 percent attendance rate before we could break even, so that even with a full house at every performance, the profit was minimal. When I expressed my concerns to George, he would only respond – and with conviction, "Eva, you don't have to worry. Only a bayonet in front of the theater will keep anyone away. Crowds of people will be clamoring to see these performances!"

So we took *West Side Story* to Berlin, Hamburg, Munich, and Stuttgart. George had a wonderful sense of humor, but, in this case, he was dead wrong, and we lost our shirts – to the tune of $20,000 each – which in those days was a considerable sum. Not only did we lose a lot of money, we also had to cancel a number of performances. As it turned out, the cultural proclivities of German audiences of the moment were totally out of sync with a production of this type – as was the country's political situation at that time. So along with our contractual issues, the entire tour turned into an absolute disaster.

From a cultural perspective in 1961, the theater-going audience in Hamburg, Munich, and Stuttgart had a difficult time relating to an American musical that portrayed gang violence and warfare. After all, this was an American issue and part of American culture, and the theaters, which ended up being less than half full in every city, echoed that sentiment.

More importantly were the events in Germany at that time, and in Berlin in particular. As part of the post-war settlement between the western Allies and the Soviet Union, the country was physically divided in two: a democratic West Germany, assisted by the United States, Britain, and France, with its population able to travel easily anywhere in the world, and a totalitarian East Germany, operating under the repressive regime of the Soviet Union, which forbade personal freedoms and movement beyond its borders. Cement and barbed wire barriers, manned by state police called VoPos (short for Volkspolizei, or people's police) in East Germany, sought to keep this prison-like country in check, and shot at any person attempting to flee along its nearly 900-mile-long border.

Berlin, once the booming capital of Germany, was now an island in the middle of East Germany. The city became a microcosm of this split and was divided into four sectors: three areas in the West under control of the American, French, and British alliance, and one in the East dominated by the East German and Soviet Communist regime.

To ensure further isolation of East from West, the Communists decided in 1961 to erect a wall – known as the infamous Berlin Wall – which would last until it was torn down in 1989 as the Soviet Union began to fall apart. Built in stages, and beginning with a wire fence that was practically installed overnight between August 12 and 13, Berliners gradually saw their lives and families torn apart – much to their alarm and consternation, and despite intense protests from the West. A final 87-mile-long, gray slab of concrete that became the actual "Berlin Wall"

West Side Story poster announcing the 1961 Broadway musical's opening at the Titania Palace theater in Berlin (top left), program cover (right), and Berlin's weekly *Journal* review, "West Side in the Middle of Berlin" in the German press

Construction of the Berlin Wall – designed to stop the flow
of people from East to West – in June 1961

Some 3,400 people escape through a hole in the Berlin Wall
as it is being built near the Brandenburg Gate in 1961

View from West Berlin's Springer Verlag (Springer Publishing Company) into East Berlin, across the
mined and electrified No Man's Land separating East from West in 1971

would be completed between 1965 and 1975.

Rumors had been brewing since June that something strange was afoot, and people were anxious. It is against this political backdrop that we opened with *West Side Story* at Berlin's Titania Palast on July 29, 1961. At this point, people were still able move back and forth between East and West Berlin with some ease. With each passing day, however, their movements became more and more restricted, as the East Germans gradually installed a chain-link fence around the city, followed by concrete and metal cross-barriers, then barbed wire, and finally, the concrete wall itself. Once completed, the entire area around the eastern section of the Berlin wall had a width of about 100 feet, was filled with mines, and became known as "no man's land."

By the time the tour left Berlin for Hamburg two weeks later on August 13, 1961, the 12 to 15-foot-high chain link fence was up, and East Berliners – as well as East Germans – were no longer permitted to cross into West Berlin. Any person's last minute dash toward freedom was met with gunfire – and certain death – by the East German Volkspolizei, who watched from guard towers positioned every few hundred feet.

In the months leading up to the wall – as people still had some freedom of movement

Sign at the Berlin Wall marks "10 Years of Wall, 10 Years of Orders to Shoot, 65 Dead"

Bus passing through Checkpoint Charlie from East to West Berlin in the American sector

Watchtower with East German VoPos ready to shoot at anyone trying to escape

across the borders – I would often go into the eastern sector to visit ballet friends who danced at the Komische Oper there, but, even then, coming to East Berlin was like entering another country. Foreigners, as well as some West Germans, were allowed into East Berlin (and East Germany) – but only with special visas and through specific checkpoints assigned to them according to their nationality. As an American, I first had to enter through the American checkpoint, known as "Checkpoint Charlie," in the American sector of Berlin. I would then cross over to the East German side where my passport and a visa were required, and the VoPo border guards would run mirrors on wheels under my car, checking for smuggled goods or defectors on the return trip. Once the physical wall was up, the process became much more tedious timewise, and the VoPos were in no hurry to usher you through. I eventually decided to ditch my car and walk in on foot.

Once in East Berlin, the differences between East and West were very apparent: The mood on the eastern side of the city was far more somber than that of its western counterpart, lights were dim and streets were dark, and people spoke quietly and carefully, in constant fear of the East German police. Anyone could turn you in for any reason. In general, dancers and artists seemed to have a bit more latitude, but even they had to be careful about saying anything derogatory about the political situation, out of fear of being interrogated and sent to prison. Life in East Berlin in those days was like living under a reign of terror. What at one time had been a vibrant flow of people, activities, and ideas between East and West Berlin – especially with many people working in West Berlin and living in East Berlin – was now silence. People preferred to stay at home, afraid to come out of their houses. Along the Wall, the only activities were the vehicles going through the checkpoints, the VoPos glaring at you through their binoculars, and the occasional attempts to flee, which were usually met with disaster.

This went on for 28 years and the Berlin Wall became a political game of chess between the United States and the Soviet Union, with two American presidents giving famous speeches there, John F. Kennedy with "Ich bin ein Berliner" (I am a Berliner) in 1963, and Ronald Reagan with "Gorbachev, Tear Down This Wall" in 1987 – both making a stand against its existence. I would see the Wall go up in 1961, when I presented *West Side Story* there, and, as a resident of Berlin decades later, would also see it torn down in November 1989 at the end of the Cold War. It was a privilege to be there for both historic events.

Our high hopes for a commercial success with *West Side Story* in Germany were dashed, but the production did receive excellent critical reviews in the German press. Had we waited a year or two to present this musical in Germany, the financial outcome would probably have been different. As a result of the political turmoil, people couldn't – or chose not to – come, and the cast played to a less than a half-full house every night. In the initial days, when the chain link fence was first erected, and people were still able to go back and forth across the border, the West Berlin Senate offered East Berliners the opportunity to buy tickets to the musical with East German Marks (both currencies were already in use by then). Instead of the exchange ratio of 4 Ostmark (East German currency) to 1 Deutsche Mark (West German currency), they allowed me to trade in any East German Marks I made at a value of 1:1. That, unfortunately, didn't prove to be much help either, and both my partner, George Olivier, and I ended up by canceling half of the 14 scheduled performances.

It takes years of experience to correctly judge whether a production will succeed or not – especially if it's still an unproven entity. Even if it feels right and everything goes according to plan, the audiences you hope for can still be fickle and decide not to show up for a variety of reasons (which is disappointing) – and the

In an effort to drum up attendance for *West Side Story*, cast stars (left to right), Yvonne Othon (Anita) and Jan Canada (Maria) pose for press photos near the Brandenburg Gate in West Berlin's British sector.

Radio interview for West Side Story, Berlin 1961.

risk factor in these endeavors can be very costly. In this case, we got caught up in an historical watershed moment in Germany – and this played a big role in the tour's financial demise. We also had ourselves to blame for our inexperience. George and I should have been more in tune with what was happening politically in Germany at that time. Additional preliminary canvassing of the likes and dislikes of the German audience at that particular moment would have also been judicious. Timing – and knowing your audience – are key to these types of ventures. After all, the French are very different in temperament from the American audiences, and the German public, quite distinct from the French. Perhaps, we were also overly eager and naïve, and our contract – which was already weak – should have included fewer performances.

In hindsight, there was much to ponder, and while there were some regrets, I quickly learned from my mistakes and moved on. F. Scott Fitzgerald once said, "Being able to persist is not the most important thing. The ability to start over is." So I picked myself up and forged ahead. On a happier note, I was then surprised to learn from an ardent fan of this production – Helen Vita, a well-known West German actress – that she sat in the audience at almost every

DIE WEST SIDE STORY – EIN FLOP?
Startschwierigkeiten eines Broadway-Hits

Ruhm und Raffinement der West Side Story
Münchner Gastspielpremiere des Broadway-Musicals im Deutschen Theater

German newspaper headlines: (top) "West Side Story -- A Flop? Difficulties in Launching a Broadway Hit" / *Süddeutsche Zeitung*, Munich; (bottom) "Notoriety and Sophistication of West Side Story" / *Berliner Morgenpost*

performance throughout its entire run. She had loved the show so much, she made a point of traveling to see *West Side Story* a total of ten times during its West German tour! So go figure!

I would later relate my unfortunate tale to Leonard Bernstein himself while he was in town conducting the Berliner Philharmonic, and he couldn't believe it. There was an upside to this experience for me, however. The good press I received despite the fiasco inspired me to expand International Artists Productions into an umbrella organization under which I could develop a host of innovative projects. Because of my background in classical ballet and music (I was not particularly drawn to popular culture, though I probably would have made more money with it), it also encouraged me to pursue an eclectic variety of programs of my choosing.

So, after the *West Side Story* debacle in the early 1960s, I began looking for other interesting talent and found myself drawn to a variety of new artists, from French cabaret singers of the Edith Piaf, Juliette Greco, and Jacques Brel tradition, to cutting-edge contemporary theater. One of the early singers who toured with me with some success was the well-known French chanteuse, Barbara, who did cross over into pop music. Famous in France for her powerful voice and soulful love songs, she had performed to sold-out audiences at the Olympia and Bobino music halls in Paris, and was a big hit when I introduced her in Germany. Other similar, though lesser-known, singers would soon follow: Catherine Sauvage, Pia Colombo, and Philippe Clay.

My work was also beginning to be noticed by the German press, and I was praised for having had the courage to present an American Broadway production in Germany at such an inopportune historical moment. These flattering reviews would eventually come to the

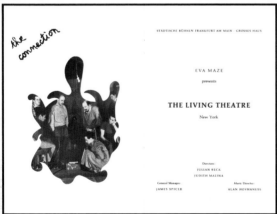

The Living Theatre program, first
European tour, 1961

attention of the 1972 Olympic Committee in Munich – with which I would forge a strong association in the years ahead.

As a result of the financial failure of *West Side Story*, my newly formed company would have gone under, were it not for a small avant-garde theatrical group from New York called The Living Theatre, which was creating a big stir at the time. I had seen the cast perform in Paris at the Festival du Theatre (Theater Festival), and thought they were intriguing and quite unusual. In the summer of 1961, about the same time that I brought *West Side Story* to Germany, I invited this unconventional theatrical group to perform there as well.

Founded as a non-traditional theatrical group by Julian Beck and Judith Malina in the late 1940s, The Living Theatre staged innovative theatrical performances of what would become known as "poetic drama" – with works of such writers, playwrights, and poets as Gertrude Stein, Jean Cocteau, Bertholt Brecht, T.S. Eliot, Federico García Lorca, and Eugene Ionesco. Living and working together as a tight-knit community in the United States and Europe, its members believed they could bring about social change with a new form of non-fictional theater based on real-life issues. Two important elements were required: the actor's total emotional and political commitment to the dramatic work, and the audience's active involvement in the play. The Living Theatre actors performed in non-traditional settings including prisons, steel mills, and slums, staging productions with what were then very controversial themes, such as drug addiction and crime in American society. They used physical effects designed to shock spectators – such as running out into the audience screaming, and performing in the nude. This new approach to acting was designed to both shake up the audience and break through what they called "the fourth wall of complacency." It would revolutionize theatrical drama.

Home for The Living Theatre, at first, was New York City. The actors then began wandering as a troupe through Europe. They were young and abrasive, and wherever they went, had a provocative and powerful effect on audiences everywhere. In 1961, I engaged them for only one production – *The Connection* – by playwright Jack Gelber, and brought them from the Paris Festival, where they were performing, to Berlin and Frankfurt, for eight shows combined. Portraying the harsh world of drug addiction in America, the play had previously opened Off Broadway at their theater, The Living Theatre, in 1959. With its highly unusual topic at the time, *The Connection* had sent shock waves through contemporary American theater. It was controversial, polarizing, and so realistic, one was hard-pressed to distinguish between theatrical performance and real life. Playwright Edward Albee declared it to be "exciting, dangerous, instructive, and terrifying, all things theater should be."

Though some people thought the play's unsavory plot and language offered an unflattering look at American society, I personally believed the drug problem was an important issue that needed to be brought to light, and applauded the actors for doing so. As a company, however, its members were disorganized and forgetful and I, as a very organized person, had a difficult time working with them. They would lose props and costumes in different places, causing last minute panic before a performance – much to the consternation of the efficient German technicians who would just shake their heads. On one occasion, the cast had even forgotten to bring along one of the most important props of *The Connection* – a toilet – which, in the play, was where the junkies got their fix. At a time of political upheaval in Berlin, we had to spend an entire day running around the city, trying to find an old, dilapidated toilet bowl – not an easy thing to do in those days.

Like a bunch of teenagers, the company was also quite defiant. For example, the United States Cultural Attaché to Germany warned them against going into East Berlin (which they ignored), and urged them to be discreet about the drug issue if they did venture across the wall. I was asked to keep an eye on them, but had no control over their behavior or decisions. They just did whatever they wanted to do, and luckily, there was no incident. They performed in West Germany several months after the *West Side Story* tour had ended – and wherever they went, were an absolute sensation.

My work as an impresario during my Frankfurt years from 1961 to 1968 would be productive, prolific, and quite successful – in sharp contrast to the inauspicious beginning with the Broadway musical.

Working at that point mostly in Germany with only one secretary, International Artists Productions was going strong. I developed a system for finding talent that worked well for me: I kept informed as much as possible about theater, ballet, and music around the world; had a constant eye on both established and emerging unusual talent; spent time researching a particular artist or company, their reputation, and experience as performers; evaluated potential box office draws as well as the interest and taste of a particular audience; learned to negotiate solid contracts; and established contacts with a variety of theatrical venues and their directors. Germany, at that time, had – and still has – a strong tradition of cultural programs that are subsidized by the German tax system in cities and towns around the country. Many of my performances were pre-sold to these municipalities, which reduced much of my own risk. I did a lot of traveling (courtesy of Pan Am), evaluating as many live stage performances as possible. During this time, I presented close to 30 different American or European companies or individual artists throughout Europe.

Once a contract was signed with the company or individual artist, my assistant and I made the travel arrangements, booked the hotels, engaged lighting or other types of technicians, and if necessary, hired musicians or an entire orchestra. The companies would travel with their own scenic design and props. Theatrical venues would, at times, change at the last minute, throwing us into a frantic search for another theater. Traveling with my artists – mostly by bus, but at times by train – I made a point to accompany them to their hotels and venues, at least for the first few performances.

Though ballet and dance remained a major focus, my interests in talent during my Frankfurt years began to expand into an even wider range of genres: flamenco, gospel, modern and contemporary dance, experimental theater, and even country-western music.

After starting out with a lesser known Spanish flamenco dancer, Tere Amorós, I was introduced to perhaps the best-known flamenco guitarist of his time, Carlos Montoya, a gypsy, or Roma, originally from Seville, with whom I would go on to tour for two years. Flamenco – with its soulful singing and clapping, guitar and castanet playing, and hypnotic tap movements – evolved as a style of music and dance out of the gypsy culture of Andalusia in the south of Spain. Carlos Montoya was a marvelous musician: Without a single prop, backdrop or artifice, he would simply walk on stage with his instrument, sit down, and captivate the audience for two hours straight with his amazing artistry and fingerwork. The only other famous guitarist to rival Montoya's playing at that time was the wonderful classical guitarist, Andrés Segovia, who was represented by Sol Hurok.

Staying in the flamenco vein, this was soon followed by a number of successful seasons in Germany, and other European cities with two leading Spanish flamenco dance companies, Luisillo y su Teatro de Danza Española, and Baile Español de Antonio Gades. A gifted dancer, choreographer and, in the 1970s, the Artistic Director of the Spanish National Ballet, Gades, in particular, was already well-known in Spain

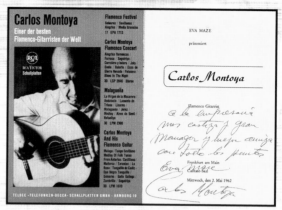

Virtuoso flamenco guitarist Carlos Montoya, with whom I forged a long friendship

Program cover of the Spanish dance company, Luisillo, April 1964

95

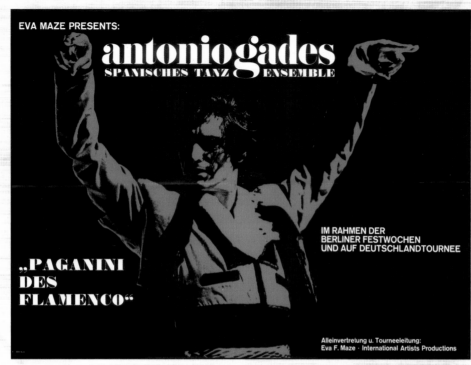

Called "Flamenco's Paganini," Antonio Gades and his dance ensemble, Ballet Nacional Española,
helped popularize Spanish flamenco all over the world and toured with us for many seasons.

and Europe, having appeared in several Spanish films with dance adaptations from Carmen and
Manuel de Falla's ballet, *El Amor Brujo*. Touring often with a large company of 12 dancers, two
guitarists and a singer, he was committed to promoting flamenco around the world. A virtuoso
of intricate flamenco footwork and tap, Gades would mesmerize audiences everywhere, and
watching him perform was an absolute treat. He was an amazing artist, and we were fortunate
to tour together for a total of six seasons throughout Europe, both in the1960s, and again in the
late 1970s.

During this time, I also took on the Dublin Festival Company, a theatrical group
recommended to me by an English impresario. Their lead actress, Siobhan McKenna, was well-
known internationally, and I thought this company would appeal to the German audiences –
and it did. We arranged for the productions of *Playboy of The Western World* by John Millington
Synge and *Mrs. Warren's Profession* by George Bernard Shaw to be performed in Germany in

Interview with Siobhan McKenna (left) during the production of *Playboy of the Western World*

McKenna and Dowel Donnelly in John Millington Synge's play

English. The director of the Frankfurt Opera, whose name was Harry Buckwitz, gave me some valuable advice at the time: He thought I had "good taste" in the performing arts, but urged me to be selective and not to present too many different productions at once. I would heed these words carefully throughout my entire career, but in looking back on the number of companies I handled simultaneously in those years, am not sure I followed his advice too closely. I was on a mission, totally committed to what I was doing.

My closest brush with popular music was perhaps an association that I forged for three years with an American promoter of country-western music from Alabama, who was introduced to me by the American Cultural Attaché at the Embassy in Bonn. He was interested in touring different country-western singers in the U.S. military-based clubs throughout Germany. In 1961, there were about 10 million military personnel deployed over dozens of bases throughout West-Germany. I was familiar with the one in Frankfurt, where my daughter Stephanie was attending

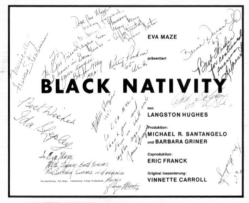

Program signed by African-American
gospel singer Marion Williams and
cast, during one of our two German tours
of *Black Nativity*, by poet-playwright
Langston-Hughes, in the 1960s

high school. Though I had little knowledge about (or interest in) country-western music, this particular promoter didn't have a license to practice in Germany. Since I did, we made an agreement for him to work under my license – which was completely legal in Germany. I never actually saw any of the performances – something I sincerely regret to this day. I later learned that the singers on tour during those three years included country-music royalty: Johnny Cash, Hank Williams, Jr., Loretta Lynn, and June Carter Cash. I did, however, end up making my first serious amount of money, enough to buy some land along the coast of the Ionian island of Corfu in Greece, where we would spend our summers for the next 25 years.

I also became interested in gospel music. I learned about a work that was being performed Off Broadway at the 41st Street Theatre in New York City called *Black Nativity*, written by African-American poet-playwright Langston Hughes, with Marion Williams, a well-known gospel singer, as the lead. Given all the social and political upheaval in the United States then – which we were very much aware of as a family, despite the fact we had been living the entire time overseas – I thought it not only timely, but also important to introduce this show in Europe. Plus I knew it would be a hit with European audiences everywhere because of its deep and exuberant gospel genre, which was still relatively unknown there.

The historical significance of the production would not be lost on the Europeans either. Aware of the social upheavals in the United States, they were seeing the first black Broadway play ever written by a successful African-American playwright, being performed by an all-black cast of singers; were hearing a type of music – gospel – that was relatively new to them; and were listening to a familiar story of the Bible – the birth of Jesus – told in a novel and compelling way through gospel-style Christmas carols and songs.

Though it only had a short run on Broadway in 1961, *Black Nativity* was very well received in Europe, and I ended up touring the company with much success for three years straight through the cities and towns of Germany, Switzerland, Belgium, Holland, Austria, and Lichtenstein. Connections between performances were often very tight. In one instance, we had to schedule a charter plane between Zurich and Düsseldorf on the German Lufthansa Airlines, in order to get the cast to a second show on the same day (most of their travel was done by bus). The lead singer, Marion Williams, who was very superstitious, at first, was afraid to board the flight – though she finally relented after much coaxing by the cast. We arrived just in time for the performance, and as in all the other cities, the curtain calls were long and loud.

Black Nativity performed close to 30 times under my auspices in Europe during those three seasons. On one occasion, I had the good fortune of meeting, in person, the poet and original narrator of the 1961 Broadway production of *Black Nativity*, Langston Hughes. Then in his late fifties, he had come to see one of the performances. A true Renaissance man, Hughes was a prolific poet, social activist, novelist, playwright, columnist, essayist, and children's book author. In the Broadway production, he had interspersed his own poetry with the songs and hymns of the musical, and his original role of narrator had now been taken over by a member of the touring cast. He liked the show, and approved of it – and I couldn't have been happier.

As a result of *Black Nativity's* success, I decided to take another black gospel group on tour in 1969, *Trumpets of the Lord*. Based on a musical by Vinnette Carroll, and adapted from the verse sermons of *God's Trombone* by James Weldon Johnson and gospel hymns, the show turned into a religious revival meeting that had jubilating audiences dancing in the aisles. At every performance in Germany, this most uplifting play – which had opened and closed at the Brooks Atkinson Theatre in New York within seven days – received an enthusiastic reception throughout Germany. One incident would unfortunately mar this otherwise thoroughly

Program cover of the revival-like *Trumpets of the Lord*, which featured the Christmas story through gospel-style songs and carols. This uplifting show had audiences out of their seats, clapping and dancing at every performance.

enjoyable experience: the arrest of one of the singers on the Reeperbahn red light district in Hamburg, who, despite our urgent pleas to the police, was not allowed to return with the cast to the United States. The musical, however, was a huge success.

As my experience and connections grew, so did my familiarity with the theater-going public in Germany.

I learned, for example, that they were receptive to both contemporary dance – in particular the José Limón Dance Company, Swedish Cullberg Ballet, and Bella Lewitzky Dance Company – as well as traditional ballet, such as the highly respected Finnish National Ballet and the American Ballet Theatre, where the brilliant Russian-born dancer, Michael Baryshnikov, was lead dancer. That they were drawn to classical Greek tragedies such as Sophocles' *Oedipus Rex*, and Aristophanes' *The Birds* – even though both were performed in ancient Greek by the Theatro Technis of Athens. That they were intrigued by the exotic plays of Japanese Kabuki. That they loved folkdance rhythms, such as those of the lively Rapsodia Romana (Romanian Rhapsody) – Romania's then official folkdance troupe – as well as the more subdued dance forms of India's Kathakali Dance Theater. That they welcomed American contemporary works translated into German, such as Robert Ward's finest opera, *The*

Crucible (based on Arthur Miller's original play). And that they liked the physical engagement of avant-garde experimental theater, similar to that of Polish director, Jerzy Grotowski, whose "Laboratory" productions were held in churches and cathedrals. The eclectic European taste in the performing arts was inspiring, and I went along with it, introducing these groups (among many others) to the German and European public. The positive reviews from the German and European press – as well as the continuous warm welcome by the public – only reinforced my convictions that I was on the right track. As far as the groups themselves, it was an absolute pleasure working with them as well.

An impresario will almost always develop a good relationship with the companies or artists he or she represents. There are times, however, when you have to sever your ties with them, at least temporarily. Lar Lubovitch's dance company unfortunately presented one of those situations in the early 1970s. A very gifted dancer and choreographer, who has had a huge impact on dance, and more recently in the world of ice-dancing, Lar Lubovitch's demands as an artist at the time of our first tour in Germany were impossible for me or the theatrical managers to meet. He needed four hours of rehearsal time prior to each performance – which was just not doable, given our tight schedule. We were per-

India's Kathakali Dance Theater performing the epic poem, *Mahabharata*.

Romanian Rhapsody: the premier national folk dance ensemble of Romania in the 1960s

forming in different towns every night and needed to factor in travel time. This was the only occasion in my entire career when it became necessary to break a contract. We would, nevertheless, work out our differences in later years, and reconnect in the 1980s for tours throughout Germany and Europe that lasted six successful seasons (Fall 1987 to Spring 1990).

There are other situations, too, when the signing of an agreement with a company or an artist depends on meeting some more unusual demands. One such example was the Harkness Ballet, which I took to Romania. Rebecca Harkness, the founder of the group and then in her 70s, insisted on having her entourage – including her maid and personal ballet trainer – travel with her, even though she was not a dancer. Special accommodations and a personal studio had to be in place at every venue so that she could take her private classes (which she often did on toe) with her trainer there. This, of course, came at an additional cost to my company.

Then there are those situations where you are thrilled to be representing an artist or a company, and despite a series of successful tours and a good relationship, the company decides, for whatever reason, to sign up with another impresario or manager, and move on. Alvin Ailey was a case in point.

In the late 1950s, upon the advice of a friend, I attended the performance of a young African-American Company, named after its founder, Alvin Ailey. The event was being held at New York's 92nd Street Y, a popular performance site for many artists on the Upper East side of the city. I had met Alvin Ailey once in the mid-1950s when he was dancing with Carmen de Lavallade in the Broadway show *House of Flowers*, starring Pearl Bailey and Diahann Carroll. A beautiful dancer, Lavallade had been a school friend of Ailey's, and in his early years, had introduced him to Lester Horton, who owned a racially mixed dance studio in Hollywood – the first of its kind in the United States.

At Horton's school, Ailey was exposed to a variety of dance techniques, including classical ballet, modern dance, jazz, and Native American dance – all of which would impact his own choreography in the future. Heavily influenced by his African-American roots and the Black experience, and less interested in the choreography of the established modern dancers of the day (i.e. Martha Graham, Doris Humphrey, and José Limón etc.), Ailey decided, upon Horton's death, to create his own multi-ethnic company in 1958 under the name of Alvin Ailey American Dance Theater. He would become a prolific choreographer for his own very successful company

Poster of The Alvin Ailey American Dance Theater performing in Belgium during one of our two very successful tours in Germany and other European countries

Program cover, performance credits' page, and portrait of Alvin Ailey
around the time of our tours through Europe

and for others until his death in 1989. With nearly 80 works to his name, Ailey is best known for his two signature pieces, *Revelations*, a ballet set to spirituals and hymns that has become a classic, and *Cry*, a solo created as an homage to his mother on her birthday and to black women, that was originally danced to great acclaim by the very gifted African-American dancer, Judith Jameson, who would eventually take over the Ailey company.

When I first saw the Alvin Ailey American Dance Theater perform – Ailey was still getting his company organized – I knew immediately it was headed for success. We ended up working together on two significant tours: one in 1965, the company's first big European tour, which I represented in Germany and took to eight cities, including Hamburg, Berlin, Frankfurt, Stuttgart, and Munich. The other, in 1967, when I presented Ailey for two weeks in Germany, Belgium, Portugal, Switzerland, and Austria. We did press and television in every city, and were met with tremendous enthusiasm and applause everywhere. In Hamburg alone – on its first tour in Germany – the Alvin Ailey Dance Theater received an astounding 80 curtain calls one evening (we counted them)! The public just wouldn't leave. Then, with Judith Jameson joining the ensemble in 1965, and becoming part of the second tour, her performance of *Cry* brought down the house nightly. When each evening closed with the powerful performance of *Revelations*, the audiences went crazy. With such talents as Judith Jameson, Dudley Williams, and Takako Asakawa, this was always an exciting company to watch – and, with the new dancers who have joined the company since then, it remains so to this day.

A consummate artist, who was supremely talented both as a dancer and choreographer, Ailey could be a bit temperamental, though he always treated me with respect. Speaking several languages himself, he would address me in French as "Madame Maze"– even though we were both American. He would complain about the performance schedule, the "one-night-stands" as he called them, where the company would have to perform in a different city or town every day, which can be taxing on dancers. My desire, nonetheless, was to give them as much exposure as possible – which they liked as well.

So it was a double-edged sword, and one that, in the end, allowed the Alvin Ailey Dance Theater of the 1960s, and their dancers, to perhaps become better known in Europe than they were in the United States – whether it was through my efforts or those of other impresarios they enlisted. My only regret is that I was not able to do more tours with them in subsequent years. As they grew, they sought out other managers and representation, but I would always find solace knowing that I had launched them in Germany, and that we both had experienced this historic performance with 80 curtain-calls at the Schauspielhaus in Hamburg – something practically unheard of these days. The company would go on to found a successful ballet school of its own in New York, and is still performing worldwide with much success.

In the mid 1960s, after being accustomed to living nearly 11 years in the comfort of an organized European city Oscar was again sent by Pan Am to another country – this time to Japan, and Tokyo's Haneda Airport. We would spend our next five years in the Far East and become immersed in two entirely new amazing cultures, first in Japan for three years, then in Hong Kong. Though I didn't make a final move to Tokyo from Frankfurt until later, I initially went ahead with him to familiarize myself with our new surroundings and find housing.

Upon our arrival in Tokyo in 1965, we were immediately met by an earthquake – not a terrible one, but one that nevertheless sent small shockwaves and fear through the entire island of Honshu, on which Tokyo is located. Though underground rumblings were common then (and still are, as much of the country sits at the intersection of three continental plates that grind against each other and periodically build up pressure), this was the only time we actually experienced an earthquake during the three years Oscar and I lived in Japan. Frightening as it was, it was still rather mild, and we weren't injured.

Because of my professional commitments in Germany, it would be a while until I was able to leave Frankfurt entirely, and Oscar and I decided instead to commute back and forth between Germany and Japan, via Pan Am, of course. Though difficult as it was, this arrangement allowed me to both plan and travel for my upcoming productions and, when possible, also spend time with my family in Japan. Our daughters would come over on their school breaks, and we made a point of traveling together as a family throughout the country during those weeks.

By 1965, our children were no longer physically living with us: My younger daughter, Lauri, was attending boarding school at the French Lycée in Tokyo, and would eventually receive her French baccalaureate degree from the University of Strasbourg in France and go on to the University of Pennsylvania. My other daughter, Stephanie, had started college at the American College (now University) of Paris after attending Frankfurt American High School in Germany, and would graduate from Georgetown University in Washington, DC.

Views from our homes in Asia, late 1960s to early 1970s:
the Shibuya-Ku, Tokyo, neighborhood (left), and the Hong-Kong skyline (right).

We found a modern western-style apartment in the upscale neighborhood of Shibuya-Ku. I remember how confusing it was to navigate this heavily populated, yet fascinating city, because so many of the streets had no names, and cab drivers often didn't know their way around them. I loved walking through the Ginza, Tokyo's shopping district, having tea at the Okura Hotel, visiting Kyoto, and shooting the rapids of the Gifu Nagara River as a tourist with my family. I learned about Japan's elegant culture and arts, from its intricate tea ceremonies to its tasty foods; from the art of ikebana (flower arrangement) to its rich history in ceramics; from the custom of giving gifts to hosts when you are invited for dinner, to the show of courtesy in removing your shoes when you entered their home. As an impresario, I also continued to be on the look-out for exceptional talent, traveled to the Sapporo Festival on the island of Hokkaido (where we also skied), and was able to observe a number of Kabuki and Noh companies perform in Japan. I would eventually bring one of Japan's leading Kabuki companies to Europe in 1972.

In 1968, Oscar then moved to Hong Kong for another two years. I continued to work and commute back and forth to Germany, sponsoring such artists as Konrad Ragossnig, the Austrian classical guitarist for whom I also arranged recordings with RCA, and touring with the companies and artists I had already engaged. I also continued to scout for talent.

In Hong Kong, I was able to indulge in a lifelong passion with interior design, and would renovate and decorate my homes whenever possible. Hong Kong was still a British colony and, because we lived so close to mainland China, we were exposed to an exotic world of arts and crafts, furniture, and Chinese rugs. We resided in the hills of Hong Kong Island, high above the race track, overlooking spectacular views of the mountains and city. With the city's inexpensive retail prices, we also loved to shop. For a very low price, we were able to order, through local Hong Kong merchants, beautiful embossed carpets from mainland China and Tibet that we still own to this day. Oscar was especially fond of these wool carpets, and we would have them made in Tientsin, then one of China's most prolific weaving centers, and delivered to Hong Kong. We also bought stunning modern and antique wood chests, armoires, and tables. In the early 1970s, Oscar and I also received special permission to travel to Shanghai and Beijing, at a time when China had not yet opened up to the West.

In the meantime, I was also invited by the Cultural Director of the City of Munich to produce a program for the 1972 Olympic Games.

Romanian folk dancer rehearsing for a new
international dance festival

6. The Munich Olympics

As I shuttled back and forth in 1966 between Tokyo, Japan, where Oscar was now stationed, and my business headquarters in Frankfurt/Main, Germany, I was invited by the Cultural Director (known in German as the "Referent") of the city of Munich, Dr. Herbert Hohenemser, to produce a cultural program of my choice for the 1972 Summer Olympics in Munich. Dr. Hohenemser and I had first met when the West Side Story production was making headlines in Germany and had become friends as a result of the publicity generated at that time. Our deep respect for one another was mutual and he had graciously referred to me as a "problem solver" in one of the German newspaper articles. When he approached me with this exciting offer, I accepted enthusiastically.

After spending months thinking about a project that would embody the international spirit of the Summer Games of the XX Olympiad – as well as my own role in the Olympics – I offered him the idea of creating a cultural program that would highlight the richness and diversity of folk dance worldwide, and at the same time, appeal to the international audience attending the sports events. Calling it the "International Folklore Festival," Dr. Hohenemser agreed

Stadium and sports venues, 1972 Munich Summer Olympic Games

with my proposal to feature a variety of folk dance companies (and one choir) from different countries around the world. The event would fall under the auspices of the German Olympic Committee as a joint venture with International Artists Productions, and last for 27 days from August 14 to September 10, 1972. It would also run prior to and simultaneously with the Olympic Games, and continue for several weeks after the Games were officially over.

The performances were to be held in the evening at a well-known theater-in-the-round with a 3,000-seat capacity in downtown Munich called Circus Krone. One of the largest privately owned circus venues in the world, it was founded in 1905 as an animal exhibition center, and later destroyed during the World War II bombing raids. Rebuilt in 1950, it had, by the early 1970s, become a popular site for high quality circus acts as well as rock concerts. Groups as famous as the Beatles and the Who had already entertained legions of fans there.

In addition to the performances at Circus Krone, we also decided to have some of the folk dance groups perform in Augsburg, Germany, the Olympic site for the canoeing slalom competitions and several preliminary events, as well as Kiel, where the sailing regattas were

Inside the Circus Krone theater, site of the International Olympic Folklore Festival, downtown Munich

held. I thus began searching for talent for this project in the late 1960s. The German Olympic Committee gave me the substantial subsidy of 775,000 Deutsche Marks – about $230,000 – which, at that time, was enough to cover my initial expenses, including travel, publicity, hotels, and a per diem for each of the participating dance companies. The funds would also pay all of my operating expenses for the first two weeks of actual performances at Circus Krone. Because of the enormous exposure gained by participating in this prestigious cultural event, the individual dance companies elected not to receive a salary. I followed suit, and instead agreed to a 50/50 split with the German Olympic Committee on all final box office receipts – a decision that would turn out to be to my advantage.

For the next four years – and amidst my other theatrical commitments – I spent months traveling around the world, assessing a myriad of dance companies with the intention of finding the most exciting ones for the Folklore Festival. The selection process was painstaking. Depending on the country under consideration, I would at first contact specific cultural attachés at their respective embassies. However, as word got out that I was looking for quality folk dance talent

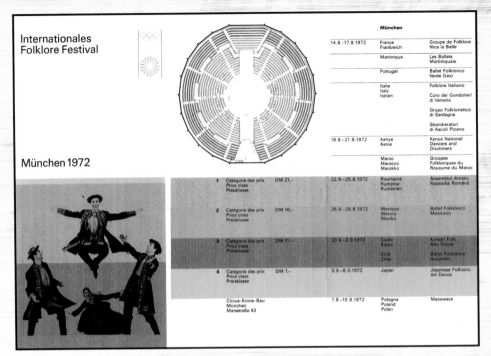

International Olympic Folklore Festival brochure with Circus Krone
theater performance schedule, seating availability, and ticket prices

Folklore festival program cover (left), and promotional flyers for advance ticket sales (right)

to bring to the Olympic Games, the foreign representatives and dance companies began to contact me directly themselves – each expressing a strong desire to be part of this venture.

After observing more than 40 dance groups on 4 continents (Asia, Europe, South America, and Africa), I narrowed my final selection down to companies from Italy, France, Portugal, Morocco, Senegal, Romania, Mexico, Chile, Korea, Japan, and Poland. Because of my desire to have the entire Folklore Festival be as diverse as possible, I then chose to alternate the programs and dance groups every four days. In the end, the International Folklore Festival would include a total of 14 companies with 720 dancers and singers from 12 nations, and evening performances of up to 4 different dance groups each.

As the Folklore Festival took shape, I also proposed to the Olympic Committee a cultural exchange between two world-class orchestras – the Munich Philharmonic Orchestra and the Japanese NHK Symphony Orchestra – as well as a series of performances in Germany by Japan's top Kabuki Theater Company from Tokyo. They would run before and after the Olympic events. The Summer and Winter Olympics were still held in the same year (a practice that continued through 1992, after which they each switched to an alternating two-year schedule). The Winter Games in 1972 were hosted by Sapporo, Japan.

For the special pre-Olympic event, the German Olympic Committee and I decided to have the Munich Philharmonic Orchestra appear at the Sapporo Winter Games in the spring of 1972, and then tour 12 Japanese cities, including Tokyo, Kyoto, Osaka, and Sapporo. In turn, the NHK Symphony Orchestra (Japan's top orchestra) would play in 12 major German cities after the Munich Summer Olympic Games had ended. Once this post-Olympics tour was over, I booked the NHK Symphony under my own auspices for additional performances to eight European countries, including Switzerland, Holland, Austria, Belgium, Finland, and England, where the BBC bought the rights for the orchestra to appear on television.

The NHK tour proved to be a big success wherever it went, though, once again, we were thrown into a panic when the NHK violin section arrived in London without violins for the BBC concert taping at the Royal Albert Hall. The orchestra was traveling from the Holland Festival, where it had been performing in Amsterdam, and the instruments, for some reason, never got on the plane. As always, Oscar came to our rescue by having Pan Am quickly load the instruments – which had been left at the airport – on the next flight to London, where they arrived at

Munich Philharmonic Orchestra pre-Olympic tour schedule through Japan, February 1972. Cities included Tokyo, Osaka, Hiroshima, and Sapporo.

Japan's NHK Symphony Orchestra performs at the 1972 Berliner Festwochen (Berlin Festival) and other German cities, as part of the post-Olympic festivities

the theater after the concert's first intermission. In the meantime, all of the NHK violinists had to rent instruments from the London Conservatory, but they were finally able to resume playing with their own violins by the second half of the program.

Throughout the tour with the NHK, European audiences always seemed surprised to learn that the orchestra's repertoire was quite westernized, and that its programs included far more European composers (Brahms, Tchaikovsky, Sibelius…) than Japanese masters, such as Toshiro Mayuzumi – known for his ballet, *Bugaku* – or Takemitsu Toru, who wrote music for the western scale.

As for the Kabuki Theatre of Japan, which performed for four consecutive nights at the Gärtnerplatz Theater in Munich prior to the Olympic Games, this type of theater proved to be an entirely new experience for the German public, as it had never been presented in Germany before. Those who attended the performances (the press and public) found Kabuki captivating, though somewhat confusing, since all the roles – even those of the female characters – are traditionally performed by men. From the time they are children, the Kabuki actors (men and boys) receive highly-specialized training in this most unique Japanese theatrical art form, which is passed on in a family from generation to generation. Kabuki dramatizes stories that are set in the Feudal Period of Japan (14th – 19th century), and uses music, voice, masks, and richly embroidered costumes to convey them. These stories can last for hours – or even up to a full day.

For four consecutive evenings, the Kabuki group performed the early 18th century classic, Chúshingura, an 11-act play about 47 masterless samurai (or ronin), who avenge the forced suicide of their master, Hangan, on the person responsible for his death, the Shogun Morono. Because it was delivered entirely in Japanese and had a complicated plot, I hired a German actor from Berlin's Schiller Theater, Manfred Greve, to narrate the story in German during each performance. I was pleased to see that both the German press and the public were impressed with the play – and considered this to be a good omen for the folk dance festival that soon would follow. Manfred would later become my assistant and tour many theatrical productions throughout Germany on my behalf.

In addition to the Folklore Festival, the Kabuki presentations and the NHK Symphony / Munich Philharmonic Orchestra exchange in Europe and Japan, one more artist – handled in conjunction with the Kammerspiele (City Theater) of Munich – was added to my list of Olympic cultural events: Jerzy Grotowski and his Laboratory Theater (Teatr Laboratorium).

KABUKI

Im Rahmen des Kunstprogrammes der Spiele der XX. Olympiade München 1972

Veranstalter: Eva F. Maze

In Zusammenarbeit mit Kokusai Bunka Shinkokai unter der Schirmherrschaft der Japanischen Botschaft der Bundesrepublik Deutschland

Staatstheater am Gärtnerplatz

Japanese Kabuki actors in a fighting scene from feudal play, Chunshingura

A male Kabuki actor prepares for a female role in Chunshingura

Der Schleier ist gelüftet: Jerzy Grotowskis „armes Theater" in München

Die Bühne wird zum Gotteshaus

Das Publikum wird zur Kulisse

Grotowski gastiert in der Ruine der Allerheiligen-Hofkirche

Polnisches „Theaterlaboratorium" in der Hofkirche

Sonst kommt Grotowski nicht

Über das wohl exklusivste Ereignis im olympischen Kunstprogramm, des Polen Jerzy Grotowskis mehrtägiges Gastspiel in der Allerheiligen-Hofkirche an der Münchner Residenz, ab die Veranstalterin Eva Maze gestern erste Informationen. Die um 1830 nach Entwürfen von Klenze erbaute, 1944 zerstörte Kirche wurde in drei Monaten um 55 000 Mark soweit präpariert, daß darin auch in

Zukunft Theater gespielt werden kann.

Bei Wein und trockenem Brot berichtete Eva Maze mit entwaffnendem Charme, wie schwierig es war, Grotowski nach München zu kriegen. Voriges Jahr im November kam er auf Einladung der Kammerspiele, um einen geeigneten Spielort zu suchen. Grotowskis „Theaterlaboratorium" (14 Personen, davon sieben Schauspieler) tritt nie in Theatern auf. Intendant Everding bot 70 mögliche Spielstätten an, darunter 40 Kir-

chen, einige Straßenbahndepots, Kasernen, Museen, einen Bierkeller. Grotowski, dem von alledem nichts zusagte, reiste enttäuscht ab.

Kammerspiel-Dramaturg Wolfgang Zimmermann hatte sich „hereinlegen lassen": Die Idee, Grotowski die Allerheiligen-Hofkirche zu zeigen, ließ er auf Grund einer Falschinformation („Man sagte mir, die wird abgerissen") wieder fahren. Als Retterin in der Not wurde Eva Maze engagiert: Grotowski kam noch einmal nach München, sah die Kirche und war entzückt.

Eine Kirchenruine für Grotowski

Gastspiel des Theaterlaboratoriums fast geplatzt

Ins Jetzt beschworene Apokalypse

Mysterienspiel von Jerzy Grotowski in der Allerheiligen-Kirche in München

Von unserem Korrespondenten

München, 24. August

Mysterienspiele galten und gelten in unserer Zeit als Geheimtip. Sie sind keineswegs selten. Um zu schweigen von Vereins- und Schulaufführungen, erinnert an Max Melis Apostelspiel, Hofmannsthals „Jedermann", an Strawinskys „Sinflut" und Noah Greenbergs Aufführung von „Daniel in der Löwengrube" mit mittelalterlichen Musikinstrumenten. Das moderne Theater hat uns, oft bis zum Überdruß, mit mystischen, kultischen, urtümlichen und obszönen Darstellungen an den Rand der Verzweiflung gebracht. 1959 begann der damals 26jährige polnische Schauspieler Jerzy Grotowski mit einer Truppe zu experimentieren. 1965 ging er mit seinen Schülern nach Breslau, wo ihm ein kleiner Saal zur Verfügung gestellt wurde: sein inzwischen weltberühmt gewordenes Theaterlaboratorium „Institut zur Erforschung des Schauspielers".

Grotowski läßt ohne Masken, ohne Kostüme, ohne Kulissen und fast ohne Requisiten spielen. Er predigt Disziplin und Askese. Der Ausdruck liegt im Körper, in der Stimme, in Sprechgesang

vor der Kirchentür bei zehn Grad Celsius 20 Minuten warten ließ, bis er es in den hohen kalten Raum ließ, den ein am Boden stehender Scheinwerfer sparsam erleuchtete.

Das Kirchenschiff ist der Schauplatz. Man gewahrt fünf Männer und eine Frau. Sie liegen oder kauern am Boden. Das Stück heißt „Apocalypsis cum figuris", die Figuren heißen Petrus, Judas, Lazarus, Maria Magdalena, Johannes und der Simpel. Simpel ist der Dumm-

lieben. Sie entdecken, albern oder obszön verspielt, biblische Entsprechungen. Der Mann mit dem Bart will Petrus sein. Er läßt jemanden, der den armen Lazarus (Zbigniew Cynkutis) spielen möchte, den Heiland sein. Er läßt sich von der Hure, die natürlich die Maria Magdalena (Elisabeth Albahaca) spielen muß, die Füße waschen. Judas, der Verräter (Zygmunt Molik) erkennt diesen Lazarus als Christus an. Das geht dem Petrus aber zu weit, also überträgt er die Christus-Rolle dem Simpel, was brüllendes Gelächter erregt: Ein grober Scherz führt zur Wiederkunft Christi. Auf den Schultern dieses Christus reitet Petrus durch die Kirche.

Im zweiten Teil erlischt der Scheinwerfer. Petrus bringt Kerzen. Es kommt zum Abendmahl, das Brot wird geteilt, es kommt zu einer Orgie. Der Simpel das Lamm, wird geopfert, das heißt niedergeschlagen, um seinen Körper beginnt ein orgiastischer Tanz. Petrus zelebriert die lateinische Messe. Aber der Tempel wird zur Räuberhöhle, und das gibt dem wieder aufgestandenen Simpel Gelegenheit, die Händler aus dem Tempel zu treiben, als letzten Johannes (Stanislaw Scierski), der sich

Olympia 72 München Kiel

Polish experimental theater director, Jerzy Grotowski (bottom left), participates in the 1972 Munich Olympics cultural events on condition that his play, *Apocalypsis Cum Figuris*, be performed in the ruins of Munich's Allerheiligen Church. The headlines, "The Stage as House of God" (top), "The Audience as Scenery" (second from top), "Grotowski Will Otherwise Not Attend"(center left), "A Church Ruin for Grotowski", and "Into the Summoned Apocalypse" (bottom right) attest to his controversial demands.

116

Grotowski was an avant-garde Polish director, who was making an impact on contemporary theatrical communities around the world. Eccentric and difficult, his productions were controversial, and his personal style was criticized by the press. His performances, however, were very much in demand wherever he staged them, and they always sold out. A self-styled guru, he believed – like New York's Living Theater – in the complete immersion of both actors and audience in a play, or what he called the "total act" of theater. He limited the size of his audience, which he would integrate into non-traditional theatrical settings, such as churches, factories, prisons, and even a crematorium. This meant that the number of people admitted to each performance was finite.

In Munich, where Grotowski directed one of his signature plays drawn from the Bible, *Apocalypsis Cum Figuris*, in a church called Allerheiligen Hofkirche (All Saints Church), no more than 50 adults and 100 students were admitted to each performance at a time – and performances were limited to only one a day. He would stand at the entrance to the church, carefully counting each person as he or she entered, and then, much to everyone's consternation and protests, shut the doors once all the seats inside had been filled. Because of the biblical connotations of this particular play (the Last Supper), bread and wine were served at the press conferences that preceded the play. Grotowski's idiosyncrasies led to some ridicule in the press, but the demand for his productions remained so strong that he became one of the highlights of the cultural events of the Munich Olympic Games.

In the early planning stages of the International Folklore Festival, we were still living in Tokyo and Hong Kong, and I was doing a lot of traveling, but in 1970, Oscar was re-assigned to Germany – this time to West Berlin – to help expand Pan Am's Internal German Service (IGS).

Pan Am was then at its pinnacle: With its famous slogan as the "World's Most Experienced Airline," it had inaugurated the Boeing 747 and revolutionized wide-body air travel, introduced the first computerized booking system for airline and hotel reservations (PANAMAC) that it developed with IBM, and designed a new terminal building at John F. Kennedy Airport – the Worldport – which allowed people to board and disembark flights by covered movable stairs called "ramp stairs." This eventually led to the jet bridge that connects the gate to the plane, and both are still in use worldwide at airports today. With a fleet of 150 jets flying approximately 80,000 miles daily to 80 countries around the world and destinations in Europe, Asia, Africa,

As part of the Internal German Service (IGS) post-war agreement with East Germany, a Pan Am Boeing 737 (left) lands at Tempelhof Airport, Berlin, in the late 1960s. A more modern Boeing 747 (right) takes off from Berlin a decade later.

North and South America, and Australia, the airline was then worth more than a billion dollars. Its glamour was further enhanced by the fashionable uniforms of its attractive flight attendants (known as stewardesses), who were mostly college graduates, required to be versed in several languages and basic nursing training, as well as by the high quality of its service that included on-board food inspired by Maxim's of Paris.

This elegant mode of travel contrasted in style, however, to the more mundane, yet very profitable, daily short IGS Pan Am shuttles of Boeing 727s, which connected cities in West Germany with West Berlin through specific Soviet-controlled air corridors over East German territory. Germany's national airline, Lufthansa, was prohibited from traveling these routes, as per the post-World War II agreement between the Soviets and Allies.

We moved to West Berlin, and I set up an office on the lower level of a lovely rented duplex house in Dahlem, one of the suburbs of the city close to the Freie Universität (Berlin's Free University). I then left for Munich six months prior to the start of the Olympic games and was given an office in the Cultural Office (Kulturamt) of the City of Munich. I brought my personal secretary with me from Berlin – a very capable student by the name of Martin Held – and asked my daughter Stephanie, then a fledgling photojournalist, to come over from Washington, DC, and help me with my publicity. My other daughter, Lauri, was assigned to my office as an Olympic hostess.

To promote this folklore festival and invite photo opportunities (photo-ops) from local and international print and television media, we arranged for each of the folk dance groups performing at the Circus Krone on a given evening to hold short presentations of their dance or singing program downtown at the Marienplatz in front of Munich's historic City Hall – the Rathaus – which is known for its daily "Glockenspiel" (carillon). We timed it so the dancers would appear right after the Glockenspiel finished. At specific hours of the day, 43 bells and 32 lifesize carved figures would begin to rotate to the sound of chimes through the spires and flying buttresses of the Gothic-style Rathaus, and attract crowds at Marienplatz. Those interested in purchasing tickets would be directed to the box office at the Circus Krone theater. This proved to be so popular that traffic would literally come to a standstill downtown as large numbers of curious onlookers gathered in the square to gawk – free of charge – at the festivities for 15 minutes, and, in the process, inquire about the Folklore Festival. The groups also performed at the Olympic Village, to the delight of the athletes.

Because the event attracted an international audience, I also asked my daughter, Stephanie, to introduce the nightly programs by loudspeaker at the start of each evening

Munich Rathaus (City Hall) at Marienplatz square (middle), where the Folklore Festival groups performed daily after the "Glockenspiel" (carillon) figurines finished twirling

in the three languages of the Olympic Games – English and French, and that of the host country, German. A particular evening of performances, for example, might include the countries of Italy, France, and Portugal. Italy was represented by a dance group from Sardinia, a gondolier choir from Venice, and flag wavers from the province of Ascoli Piceno on the east coast of Italy. The flag wavers would have paraded earlier that day through the Olympic Village or on the Marien-platz square. Dressed in colorful tunics and tights, 25 or so men twirling large flags adorned with medieval crosses and unicorns appeared as if they had just walked out of the Middle Ages, and the onlookers loved it! The Ascoli Piceno proved to be such a draw because of their colors and athleticism, we posted them with their flags in front of the theater every evening as the audience arrived, even when they weren't on the program.

In tandem with the international theme of the festival, the program was arranged for groups of specific dance companies to perform for four consecutive nights, then change.

Opening night was led by the group Nice la Belle from France, representing the old and traditional folk dances from the areas of Nice and the Côte d'Azur, with men in striped pants and floppy hats shouting and hopping to a slow cadence of drums around girls in layers of petticoats. This contrasted sharply with the second, more athletic Les Ballets Martiniquais from the French Caribbean island of Martinique, comprised mostly of powerful male dancers jumping to hypnotic, fast-paced drumbeats. The island of Martinique is a province ("département") of France, and its residents consider themselves both French and Martiniquais. In my travels throughout the West Indies, they were the most alluring dance company from that part of the world.

The three acts that came next were very polished: First, a troupe of more than 30 dancers, musicians, and singers from Portugal, the Ballet Folklórico Verde-Gaio, whose lively sequences and traditional choreography were precise and theatrical; then, a very sophisticated folk dance group from Sardinia, Italy, the Groupo Folklorístico di Sardegna; and finally, the official all-male Coro dei Gondolieri di Venezia (the Gondolieri Choir of Venice), singing soulful Italian songs dating back to the 15th century, that still echo through the canals of Venice today.

The second program featured two very distinct dance companies from North and West Africa, beginning with the Groupes Folkloriques du Royaume de Maroc from Morocco which, in my opinion, was one of the more captivating troupes, due to the exotic variety of its dances, drama, and costumes. Sponsored by the King of Morocco, who was pleased to have his country represented culturally at the Olympics, it was, with more than 50 participants, one of the larger contingents of dancers and musicians to appear at the festival. Drawn from cities and tribes of Morocco, it included acrobatic tumblers, women adorned in bejeweled headdresses and necklaces, and men in white costumes who performed line dance sequences, but who actually were horseback acrobats from the desert.

This was followed by the Ballet National du Senegal, from West Africa. Compared to the Moroccan dance troupe, which seemed somewhat distant and mysterious, the National Ballet of Senegal immediately connected with the audience with its pulsating drumbeats, thunderous cries of celebration, and – as per their tradition – wild, skimpily-clad dancing. Fueled by energetic songs, stilt-dancing, and incessant beating of drums, the Senegalese group concluded an evening that could have easily rivaled that of an exciting athletic competition.

Each of the companies in programs three and four were well-known, and therefore, scheduled to perform for an entire evening. First up, from Romania, was the Ansamblul Artistic Rapsodia Romana (the same company I had toured in the early 1960s), a large folk dance troupe that was accompanied by its own orchestra, a big string section, and a number of zither and pipe soloists. Based on East-European folk dances from different regions of Romania and a colorful gypsy heritage, its fast-paced music, lively choreography, and richly embroidered ethnic costumes were mesmerizing.

Four days later, audiences were treated to the Ballet Folklórico Mexicano, a very large and colorful professional ensemble from Guadalajara, already famous throughout the world. Traveling with 85 dancers, singers, and musicians, it showcased the country's rich Spanish and Indian heritage with regional dances and music from every state of Mexico, including the notable Jarabe Tapatío dance of Jalisco, the Mayan Indian Deer Dance, and Jarocho harp music from Veracruz. Along with its dazzling costumes and uplifting energy, the Ballet Folklórico performances proved to be one of the most popular folklore events.

The evening's fifth program was shared between the Korean Folk Arts Group and the Ballet Folklórico Aucamán from Chile. First up was Korea, represented by a group of women clad in white robes who danced and played their musical accompaniment – both string instruments and drums – simultaneously. Their various numbers – including a Fan Dance, a Witch's

Die spezielle Liebe Eva Mazes gilt Polen. Sie verpflichtete gleich zwei Folkloregruppen nach München

Eine Amerikanerin aus Berlin und Mutter zweier Töchter heuert Künstler aus aller Welt für das millionenschwere, internationale Kunstprogramm der Olympiade an

Der Trommeltanz wird dem Olympia-Publikum von Koreanerinnen (links) dargeboten. Das »Teufelsballett« mit seinen farbenprächtigen Masken und Kostümen stammt aus Chile

Hausfrau läßt in München tanzen

Die ernsten japanischen Herren in langen schwarzen Gewändern sagten nichts, sondern knickten nur an den Hüften ein zu einer tiefen Verbeugung. Eine quirlige Amerikanerin namens Eva F. Maze sagte „Grüß Gott", um dann ebenfalls an der Hüfte einzuknicken. Schauplatz des Zeremoniells: Flughafen München. Die Mitglieder des Kabuki-Theaters aus Japan waren zum vorolympischen Gastspiel eingetroffen, das den Auftakt bildet zu einem millionenteuren „Olympischen Kunstprogramm".

Die 44jährige Eva Maze, die die berühmten japanischen Herren an die Isar geholt hat, organisiert das „Internatio-

nale Folklore-Festival" der Olympiade. Bei dem Folklore-Auftrieb werden mit Ausnahme von Australien alle Erdteile vertreten sein. Neben dem Nationalballett aus dem afrikanischen Senegal kommen etwa Tanzgruppen aus Chile und Mexiko, Beinschwinger aus Frankreich und Polen. Koreaner werden an der Isar ebenso auftreten wie ein Gondolieri-Chor aus Venedig.

„Das Organisieren", spricht Frau Maze, „macht mir Spaß." Die Ehefrau eines Fluggesellschaft-Angestellten und Mutter zweier Töchter brachte bereits englische Tanz-Ensembles nach Indien und die Broadway-Inszenierung der

„West Side Story" nach Deutschland. Jetzt ist sie stolz darauf, daß sie ihre vertragliche Folklore-Verpflichtung mit Gruppen aus 11 Ländern und 720 Personen um mehr als 100 Prozent übererfüllt hat. Ob ihr das auch mehr einbringt, steht noch dahin. Denn welchen Teil vom Erlös Eva Maze abkassieren kann, wird von ihr so geheimgehalten wie vom Olympischen Komitee. Zur Verfügung steht zumindest ein Etat des Olympischen Komitees von 775 000 Mark. „Olympia ist für mich ein Höhepunkt", findet die Organisatorin.

Für den Höhepunkt wird das Publikum der folkloristischen Darbietungen in der

Die 44jährige Eva Maze engagierte aus elf Ländern Folklore-Gruppen. Darunter auch das berühmte »Kabuki-Theater« aus Japan

Zeit vom 14. August bis 10. September in München (Zirkus Krone) und Augsburg (Neue Kongreßhalle) bei Eintrittspreisen zwischen 7 und 21 Mark kräftig zur Kasse gebeten.

Für die innerdeutsche Folklore freilich, die nicht im Zirkus, sondern im Olympiastadion stattfindet, ist Eva Maze nicht zuständig. Hier steht den Besuchern hauptsächlich Bayrisches bevor. Allein in der Münchner Spaten-Brauerei nähen seit Wochen drei Sattler an prunkvollem Lederwerk für rund 100 000 Mark herum: Zaumzeug und Geschirr für ein Vierfachspann von Braurössern. *Gerhard Tomkowitz*

Stern Magazine's flattering article about the International Olympic Folklore Festival, "Housewife Lets Them Dance in Munich." Among others, it featured Poland's Mazowsze (top left), Korea's Folk Arts Group (center), and Chile's Ballet Folklórico Aucamán (right).

☎ 5306-1

tz

30 Pf

München, Donnerstag, 17. August 1972
Nr. 187 • 5. Jhg. • ÖS 2.— • Lit 100   B 1961

Bella Signorina

Täglich um 11 Uhr Folklore auf dem Marienplatz

tz München

Sie lächelt für München und sie lächelt für ihre Heimat. Internationaler Charme ist jetzt, wenige Tage vor dem Ereignis, das um „Olympische Spiele" nennt, an Ihrenhallen in der Landeshauptstadt anzutreffen. Die hübsche Trachtlerin ist unter italiens Sonne großgeworden und ge-

hört zur „Grupo folklorico di Sardegna", die gestern nach dem Rathaus-Glockenspiel am Marienplatz auftrat. Olympisches Kulturprogramm gibt's den jeden Tag ab 11.15 Uhr im Rahmen des internationalen Folklore-Festivals. Dabei stellen sich elf Nationen mit heimatlichen Volkskunst vor.

Attraktion auf dem Marienplatz: Die Folkloregruppe aus Sardinien

MÜNCHEN '72 ⊙⊙⊙ MÜNCHEN '72 ⊙⊙⊙ MÜNCHEN '72 ⊙⊙⊙ MÜNCHEN '72

München ist für die Spiele gut gerüstet

Die „schönsten Sportstätten der Welt"

München. „Wir könnten in der nächsten Stunde mit den Olympischen Spielen beginnen." Mit diesen Worten kennzeichnete der Chef-Koordinator des Organisationskomitees für die XX. Olympischen Spiele, Siegfried Perrey, gestern den Stand der Vorbereitung. München ist also für die Olympischen Spiele gerüstet, die nach dem Urteil von ausländischen Fachleuten „die größten Spiele in den schönsten Sportstätten der Welt" werden sollen. 122 Mannschaften mit über 9000 Aktiven werden vom 27. August an in 180 Konkurrenzen um die begehrten Medaillen kämpfen. Die umfangreichen Bauten an Sportstätten und Verkehrsanlagen, für die 1,35 Milliarden Mark ausgegeben werden mußten, waren bereits am 1. Juli abgeschlossen. Die verantwortliche Olympiabau-Gesellschaft ließ dazu vernehmen: „Nach diesem Termin brauchte nur noch aufgeräumt zu werden." Die olympischen Bauvorhaben verhalfen der bayerischen Landeshauptstadt nach dem Urteil intimer Kenner dazu, innerhalb kürzester Frist langfristige kommunale Probleme zu lösen und sich von einem „Millionendorf" zu einer Weltstadt zu mausern. Rund eine Million Besucher werden während und nach den Spielen darüber entscheiden, ob die angestrebte Wandlung zu einer „Weltstadt mit Herz" geglückt ist.

Viel bewundert wurden die mexikanischen Darbietungen der Folklore-Gruppe im olympischen Dorf.   Foto: NOP

Positive reviews in the German press of the festival's various folk dance groups performing at (Munich's) Marienplatz, including (left/top to bottom) the Grupo Folklorístico di Sardegna and Ballet Martiniquais, and (right/top to bottom) the Ballet Folklórico Mexicano, Portugal's Ballet Folklórico Verde Gaio, and (right) Nice la Belle from France, and the Ballet National du Sénégal

Dance, a Mask Dance, a Farmer's Dance, and even an Exorcism Dance – were so sophisticated, elegant, and well-received by the public and press, I ended up taking them on an additional tour through Germany after the Olympics.

In the second half of the evening, the dainty dancing of the Korean women gave way to the more masculine footwork of the Chilean Ballet Folklórico Aucamán. Drawing on Chile's rich heritage, dancers in ornate masks simulated mythological gods of the Inca Empire, while cowboys on imaginary horses parodied revered traditions of the Huaso culture.

It was, however, the last two programs that brought down the house: one, featuring virile dancers leaping around in eccentric masks and costumes from Japan; the other, showcasing lively couples swirling to fast-paced dance rhythms from Poland.

Reminiscent of the dramatic images and athletic movements of traditional Kabuki Theater (though there is no connection between Kabuki and Japanese folk dancing), the first half of the program featured a 35-member-strong folk Japanese dance troupe, the Japan Folkloric Art Dance. Founded in 1967, it was then Japan's official folk dance company. Intriguing and esoteric, its mostly male dancers bounded across the stage in surreal costumes, decorated with abstract symbols of swords, trees, animal horns, birds, and outlandish masks designed to both amuse and frighten the audience.

The festival's most impressive folk dance program, however, was the Mazowsze group from Poland, which closed the festival. This world-renowned company had already performed internationally with much success. Its dancers and musicians were highly trained and professional, its choreography, excellent and diverse, and its sets and costumes, absolutely superb. The largest company of the festival, which included 130 dancers and 35 musicians, truly reflected the rich tradition and extensive variety of Polish court and country dance rhythms – from the measured mazurkas and elegant waltzes to the spirited polkas and polonaises. Responding to encore after encore, the Mazowsze performers took the most bows of all the groups.

A 1972 newspaper article would describe me as a small, slender woman, who was responsible for the entire cultural program of the Olympics. Flattering as it was, this was not the case. I was only responsible for a few of the cultural programs, but they did get considerable attention in the press, and they did take a lot of effort to produce.

Little did people know just how much time and hard work actually went into organizing

Some of more than 100 articles in the West German press about the Folklore Festival and me at the time of the Munich Olympics. Headlines include "With 775,000 Marks Around the World: Eva Maze Buys Folk Dancing for Olympia." (left); "She Lets Nations Dance" (top); "Purchased for Olympia from Around the World" (center); "A Woman Risks Her Fortune for Olympia" (right).

this festival. With the myriad of travel arrangements that needed to be made to the countries I visited, the different foreign language contracts that required translation and negotiation, and my other tours that demanded supervision, I often wondered what I had gotten myself into. There were so many issues that needed to be resolved, I often wished I had the multiple arms of an Indian Shiva deity. So much was riding on this international event, I can honestly say that I was filled with dread each and every day right up to the first performance of the festival – and at every program change thereafter. Though the production was meticulously planned down to the most minute detail, there was always the fear that something could jeopardize its success. Yet once the first performances were underway, and positive publicity began pouring in on a daily basis, I began to relax and take comfort in knowing that practically every show sold out. The International Folklore Festival became a successful cultural highlight of the 1972 Olympic Games – and this, in the end, validated the blood, sweat, and tears that had gone into its preparation.

All of this, however, would be overshadowed by a sudden horrifying event: the Black September Massacre.

After traveling far and wide in search of top folk dance companies for such a prestigious and memorable event as the Olympic Games, after the pleasure I had fulfilling my dream of sharing the beauty of dance and culture – in this case folk dance – from around the world with visitors from every corner of the world, and after seeing audiences flock to our performances, happy and uplifted by them, it was all the more tragic for everyone to witness the horror and violence of the Munich Massacre that accompanied this 20th Olympiad.

On September 5, 1972, ten days after the Opening Ceremonies of the Summer Olympics in Munich and well into the competitions, eight members of a Palestinian group called 'Black September' broke into the Olympic Village at 4:30 a.m., and took nine Israeli athletes, coaches, and officials hostage in their apartments. The West German Olympic Organizing Committee, eager to change the Nazi militaristic image of the 1936 Olympics in Berlin, had refused to post armed security at the Olympic Village. Athletes were able to come and go as they pleased, allow-ing for easy entry to and exit from the athletic village over its fences.

Two members of the Israeli team were immediately killed and, in a subsequent stand-off between the Palestinians and authorities that lasted 18 hours, the terrorists demanded both the release of 234 prisoners held in Israeli jails and that of the two founders of a German terrorist group known as the Baader-Meinhof Red Army Faction, who, at the time, were being held in German prisons. Refusing these demands, the Germans subsequently attempted a rescue at a nearby airport, which failed. Five of the eight members of the Black September group were killed. The surviving three were captured, but later released to Libyan officials after a German Lufthansa plane was hijacked and threatened with explosives.

Eleven members of the Israeli Olympic team, including four coaches, five athletes, one judge, one referee, and one German police officer, died. In the wake of this tragedy, competition was suspended for the first time in Olympic history on September 6. A memorial service was held by more than 80,000 spectators and 3,000 athletes in the Olympic Stadium. All remaining members of the Israeli team withdrew from the games and left Munich. All Jewish athletes received additional protection, including the American swimmer, Mark Spitz, who returned to the United States with a record-setting seven gold medals before closing ceremonies, having already completed his events.

Though Willy Daume, President of the Munich Organizing Committee, thought it best to cancel the rest of the games, Avery Brundage, President of the International Olympic Committee, made the controversial decision to resume competition.

A Black September Palestinian terrorist appears on the Israeli wrestling team's balcony at the Olympic Village

16 deaths confirmed during the Massacre after the terrorists' botched escape by helicopter at the airport, and the decision to resume the Games

Memorial Service at the Olympic stadium, held in honor of the deceased members of the Israeli team

127

And despite his plea for the Games to remain unaffected by this incident, the 1972 Munich Olympics would forever be associated with this calamity, and remembered as an event that was tainted by fanaticism, pain, and much sadness.

As a result of Brundage's decision, the International Folklore Festival carried on with its daily performances as well – with one caveat: Before the start of each of our remaining programs, we stopped for a minute of silence to honor those who had lost their lives in this most unfortunate and tragic event.

2012 Munich Memorial Service and plaque commemorating the 50th anniversary of the deaths of 11 members of the 1972 Israeli Olympic team

7. Corfu

After spending more than five exhausting years working on the Folklore Festival for the Olympics – and overseeing the many other programs I was presenting in the late 1960s and early 1970s – it was time for a break. New productions weren't scheduled for another few months, and I desperately needed to relax and recharge.

In the early years, when we still lived in Frankfurt, Germany, our entire family eagerly looked forward to our summer and winter holidays in Austria, Italy, France, and Spain. My mother would often fly over from New York and join us, especially for our summer holidays on the Costa Brava in the Catalonian region of Spain. For six summers in August, we would load up our 1954 blue Buick and drive three days straight from Frankfurt through France, to S'Agaro Spain, which was then a burgeoning tourist spot a few hours north of Barcelona. Each year, we followed the same route through the Alsace region and its capital, Strasbourg, and drove through the wonderful Burgundy wine country near Lyon. There, we would stop along the road for a tasty picnic of cheese baguette sandwiches, and ripe red grapes that we had taken the liberty of picking from nearby vineyards. We would overnight in the spectacular mountains of Les Beaux

Family summer travel with our 1954 Buick   Overnighting in Les Beaux, Massif Central, France

in France's rugged Massif Central (where we enjoyed some of the most delicious honey in the world); take in some of the historic sites in the French cities of Avignon and Perpignan; and finally head down the Catalan coast of Spain through Cadaquez (home to surrealist painter Salvador Dali), Figueres, Girona, and the Costa Brava. We would unwind at the beach, see the bullfights in Barcelona, dance the Sardana in the Gothic Quarter of the city, dine on the wonderful Catalan cuisine, and enjoy some excellent wines.

Prior to relocating to Germany for Oscar's second Pan Am assignment in Berlin, friends of ours, who were Greek, suggested we visit Corfu (Kerkyra in Greek), one of the Greek islands in the Ionian Sea, located roughly four miles off the Coast of Albania, northwest of Greece. They had built a new hotel with individual bungalows on the Bay of Gouvia, and thought this beautiful and pristine Greek island, with its varied and complicated past, would appeal to us.

Steeped in mythology and a rich history going back to the seventh century B.C., Corfu had endured raids and occupations by a myriad of invaders. At one time or another, the island had fallen under Roman and Byzantine rule, become a protectorate of Venice to defend against the Ottoman Turks, and following the Napoleonic Wars, been subjected to British control in the 19th century. Each occupying force left an indelible mark on this magnificent island – particularly on its architecture. Examples of Byzantine and Venetian styles can be found in its towns and

Winter holidays in beautiful Kitzbühel, Austria   Summer vacation in S'Agaro, Costa Brava, Spain

countryside, from the beautiful Greek monastery of Paleokastritsa on the northern coast, to the curved arches of the Plaka (or central square) in the Old Town of Corfu – both of which remain major tourist attractions to this day. In 1864, under the Treaty of London, the British ceded Corfu to the Greeks, and the island finally became part of modern Greece. Corfu was then invaded once more in World War II – this time by Mussolini – and when Italy surrendered to the Allies in 1943, the Germans killed the thousands of Italians who had remained there, and deported its roughly 1,800 Jews to Auschwitz.

When we first visited Greece in 1965 (just before Oscar moved from Frankfurt to Tokyo), Corfu was a favorite destination of the European elite. Unspoiled, it had one main hotel in the central town of Corfu, limited infrastructure, three winding two-lane highways that connected the Old Town and the Port of Corfu with other smaller towns and villages around the island, many unpaved roads, and virtually no tourism. In the countryside, drinking water was collected in wells maintained mostly by the peasant population, and donkeys still carried daily necessities. There were few cars, and people got around the island mostly by mopeds.

The countryside – alternating between gold and green vistas depending on the season – was dotted with olive and cypress trees, rolling hills, a nearly 3,000 ft. tall mountain-climbing peak called Mount Pantokrator, historic ruins dating back almost 3,000 years, a few monasteries

View of the old town of Corfu (Kerkyra) in the Ionian Sea, Greece

Corfu's idyllic Pontikonissi (Mouse Island) and Panagia Vlacherna Church

and two castles. Corfu's physical setting was idyllic, and its clean sea water, endowed with a beautiful blue hue that British author and former resident, Lawrence Durrell, referred to – in his book, *Prospero's Island* – as "the heartbeat of the world itself."

At the time, few planes flew into its tiny airport – perhaps one charter a week, and tourism was just taking off. With only one hotel in town (the Corfu Palace), we chose to stay – in the early stages of our visits to Corfu – at the newly built Corcyra Beach Hotel on Gouvia Bay, east of the island. As we became more familiar with the language and customs, Oscar and I fell in love with the island's lively Greek culture and beauty, and on our third visit, decided to build a permanent summer home there.

With the money I had earned thanks to the very successful Country-Western tours with Johnny Cash and Hank Williams Jr., on the U.S. military bases in Germany (courtesy of my promoter colleague from Tennessee), we first bought a 6,000 square meter (a little over one acre) parcel of land on Corfu's northeastern waterfront in an area known as Kommeno. The following year, we drew up plans for a Mediterranean-style, whitewashed villa with a view across the Corfu Channel, toward Albania, the mountains of Macedonia and mainland Greece. At the time, Albania was a completely closed, Sino-Soviet dominated society. We called our new home "La Serenísima" (Most Serene One), and completed the house in 1969.

The legalities of owning coastal property in Greece as a foreigner were complicated, but we ended up buying this piece of land from a prominent Italian architect from Rome, Count Ernesto Azzalin, and having him design the house. He was an attractive man in his early forties, who had been asked by his uncle to sell several real estate properties he owned in Greece. Not only was Ernesto a successful architect, whose designs were known throughout Italy, Spain, and Greece, he was also charming, sophisticated, spontaneous, and emotional – in short, very Italian. I think I may have been the first person to actually purchase property from him in Greece, for he was so happy when the deal was concluded, he gave me a huge hug and a kiss. This was to be the beginning of a long friendship, both business and personal.

Ernesto and I would often meet in Rome to discuss the design and different architectural details of the house, and I always enjoyed those meetings. His energy was infectious as we sat across each other in one of the elegant Roman cafés discussing windows, walls, and arched doorways. My mind would wander, and I found myself attracted to both his enthusiasm for

Our summer home in Corfu, facing East toward Albania

this project, and to his dark blue eyes. My husband would just shake his head and tell me that I acted like an 18-year-old school girl whenever he visited us – and he was right. I was perhaps a bit infatuated with him, but whenever I was around this very suave and handsome Italian, I felt as if I were in the presence of a movie star, and was fascinated by him (he had this effect on other women as well). Of course, we were both aware that ours was primarily a business relationship, and that a host of difficult problems with the house needed to be resolved promptly. These included dealing with the more mundane yet important decisions of how best to position the property on a promontory full of rocks, access and trap drinking water, or build a quiet and reliable road to the front of the house. For me, however, it certainly never hurt to dream....

Two lots of land in this location had been up for sale, and Oscar and I had chosen the one facing the sea. From the very beginning, we were plagued by the challenge of accessing potable water, primarily because the house sat on top of a hill, and there was no underground conduit to it. At first, we decided to build a pipeline that drew water with an electric pump from a well owned by peasants close to Gouvia Bay. Because a number of people used that same well, our withdrawals were timed by a clock and measured. From there, the water flowed into another tank owned by Ernesto, close to our property, after which it was directed into a small cistern on

Moorish architectural design of our house on the Greek island

our land. This circuitous routing caused frequent water shortages, and eventually became such a nuisance – particularly with the rapid development of this area – that we ended up building a private 30 cubic-meter well on our own property, and having a truck fill it up with water once a week.

An additional complication was the access to the property itself. When the house was first completed, access to it was only through a narrow dirt road that ran past the back of the property, a short distance from our entrance. Few people used it, and the neighborhood remained relatively quiet. However, as this area expanded with new homes and a hotel nearby, the road was widened and paved to the edge of the back of our property – resulting in an increase in traffic and loud, honking noises – and we were forced to build a high stone wall along the entire back of our land to ensure additional privacy.

Then another issue arose around our jetty. We had built a strong, wooden 100-foot jetty that extended from the rocky beach below us out into the sea. It belonged to our property, but because of a law in Greece stating that everyone has the right to use any construction built over water – especially if it can be accessed by boat from the sea – our jetty became a magnet for swimmers, sailors, and boaters, and was always crowded. Since it was an attractive and well-maintained dock, there were at times so many people and boats gathered around it during the day, the only quiet moments we had as a family for a private swim were early in the morning or late in the evening. Corfu also has a heavy rainy season which, in those days, could cause considerable damage to the property, and in the 20 plus years we lived on the island, the jetty would be completely destroyed and rebuilt three times.

On a more positive note, we quickly adjusted to a comfortable Greek summer life on Corfu and came to love its food, architecture, and music – as well as the charismatic nature of the Greeks themselves. Our friends were drawn from an eclectic international group of Corfiotes, Greeks from Athens and the rest of the mainland, members of various foreign services and the U.S. State Department, Greek royalty, members of the U.S. Mediterranean 6th Fleet that occasionally patrolled the area, and professional or retired families from around the world. Beautiful sailboats anchored in our cove for lunch, huge motor cruisers, including several that belonged to the Onassis family (one of Greece's premier shipping magnates) stopped for the occasional swim, and crews scoured locations for upcoming films. *The Greek Tycoon* with Anthony Quinn and Jacqueline Bisset, for example, was filmed on the island, thrilling my older daughter, when she had a chat with Anthony Quinn one afternoon as he swam up to our jetty and invited her to be an extra in the film.

The blue waters of Paleokastritsa on the western coast of Corfu

We bought a small red motorboat and waterskied, gathered often for a *vanílya* (a Greek traditional drink with a scoop of vanilla caramel in a glass of water) under the Venetian arches of the *Plateia* square downtown, celebrated Greek holidays with ouzo and retsina (and smashed a few dishes as well), danced Greek folk dances to bouzouki music in the evening, and learned to make the local moussaka with potatoes and a delicious souvlaki. We took many family outings to other parts of the island, including to what was then an unspoiled rocky beach that lies below the famous Paleokastritsa Monastery, and has since become a favorite destination spot for tourists. There, we had the luxury of choosing for lunch a fresh lobster, fished that morning out of the chilled waters of nearby coves. We also learned enough Greek to communicate with the caretakers of our house and buy groceries at the local Tzavros market – including specialties like Greek goat feta, kalamata olives, melitzanosalata (eggplant dip) and taramosalata (fish roe). Their fresh, creamy Greek yogurt and rice pudding with cinnamon were already bestsellers 50 years ago.

Oscar enjoyed working in the garden, and when he had a few days off while I was on tour, he would be the one to oversee the upkeep of the house. As tourism increased on the island, so did the flights and, instead of going through

Scenes of the port in the old town of Corfu (top), the Venetian *Plateia* square (middle), and a residential area with shops and cafés (bottom)

Photo of the 6th Fleet's U.S.S. John F. Kennedy aircraft carrier, signed by Admiral Earl Yates

Navy personnel of the U.S.S. John F. Kennedy prepare to tow our red motorboat to the Port of Corfu for minor repairs

Athens, which we did in the first few years, Olympic Airlines started direct shuttles to Corfu Airport several times a week, using older style DC4 and DC6 propeller aircraft. Once my husband relocated back to Germany from the Far East, it was very easy for him to hop on a flight in Berlin or Frankfurt, and arrive in Corfu a few hours later.

My daughters enjoyed the island's social life (clubbing, dancing, waterskiing…) when they were on vacation from school and college, and mingled easily with its young, international crowd. As a family, we entertained a lot, welcoming people from all walks of life, including lawyers, engineers, students, royalty, business people, and even a U.S. admiral, who happened to be in town on one occasion with the 6th Fleet's USS Kennedy.

Built in Newport News, Virginia, the U.S.S. John. F. Kennedy aircraft carrier had been christened by Caroline Kennedy, daughter of the late President, and launched in 1967 as part of the 6th Fleet that patrolled the Mediterranean region. The ship would complete maneuvers throughout the area, including the Ionian Sea, and at times dock close to the port of Corfu, where it would send one of its destroyers into the harbor for several days. Of course, whenever this happened, it was a big event on the island.

On one such occasion, and a few days

after a severe storm had damaged and almost sunk our own small motorboat, we saw a cruiser pull up to our jetty and several men in uniform emerge from it. Curious to see who they were, we went down to greet them and learned that they were officers of the American destroyer anchored in the harbor, who were taking a tour of the island. We also found out that Admiral Earl Yates, the original commander of the USS Kennedy, was in town, and spontaneously decided to throw our first big party for him, and all the senior officers and their wives. We invited everyone we knew in our neighborhood and the town of Corfu, and the party was a huge success. In return, Admiral Yates graciously sent several midshipmen the following day to our jetty, attached our damaged little red motorboat to the back of their cruiser, and tugged it to their destroyer in port, where it was repaired by qualified mechanics. It was then delivered back to our jetty in perfect condition a few days later. Perhaps in today's world, some might look askance at this type of good deed, but in those days, it was viewed favorably by the public at large, American or Greek, and went a long way toward promoting good will and valuable public relations. And needless to say, we were thrilled! Several weeks later, we also received a lovely photo of the USS Kennedy signed by Admiral Yates, thanking us for the party.

These unexpected events on Corfu made for some wonderful memories of our summers there….

We also had a group of interesting neighbors, some of whom became good friends for a number of years. They included Princess Sophie and Prince George of Hanover and their children, who had a summer home nearby. We would often visit with one another.

Princess Sophie of Greece and Denmark was one of four sisters of Prince Philip, Duke of Edinburgh, and Queen Elizabeth's consort. Both Prince Philip and Princess Sophie – two of five children of Prince Andrew of Greece and Denmark and Princess Alice of Battenberg – had been born in Mon Repos, the Greek royal family's summer residence on Corfu. In our early years on the island, Mon Repos was still the summer home of King Constantine II of Greece, who lived in Athens. Prince George of Hanover was a brother of Queen Frederike of Greece and a grandson of the German Emperor, Wilhelm II.

Princess Sophie had a very pleasant, easy-going personality and sense of humor, and was not well-known to the general public. She led a rather quiet, yet unusual life that alternated between royal palaces and simple residences, right up to her death in 2001. She was warm and

Our Corfu neighbors and friends,
Princess Sophie and Prince George
of Hanover

Princess Alice of
Battenberg, who became a
nun. She was the mother of
Princess Sophie of Greece
and Denmark and Prince
Philip, Duke of Edinburgh.

unassuming, and liked to be called "Sophie." As a child, she had lived mostly in Athens and Paris with her mother, Princess Alice of Battenberg, (her parents were separated). She married twice: first in 1930, at the age of 16, to Prince Christoph of Hesse, a German royal and great-grandson of Queen Victoria, who would become a Nazi member of the German Luftwaffe (Air Force) during World War II, and die in an airplane crash over Italy in 1943; then, to Prince George of Hanover, a descendant of the German House of Hanover and an educator, who later became a member of Germany's International Olympic Committee (IOC). He would die in 2006 at the age of 90.

Sophie's mother, Princess Alice, herself had been a remarkable woman. A great-granddaughter of Queen Victoria, she was deeply devoted to charitable and spiritual causes. She was born almost deaf, and later diagnosed with a mental illness, from which she recovered in a Swiss sanatorium. During World War II in Athens, she worked for the Red Cross, setting up soup kitchens and orphanages, and sheltering Greek Jewish refugees – for which she received a Holocaust Memorial Yad Vashem Award. In 1949, she founded a Greek Orthodox nursing order of nuns called the Christian Sisterhood of Martha and Mary – and became a nun herself (the order no longer exists). After quietly living her last two years at Buckingham Palace in London with Queen Elizabeth and Prince Phillip, she was laid to rest in 1969, and later transferred, as per her wishes, to the Convent of Saint Mary Magdalene on the Mount of Olives in Jerusalem in 1988.

When we met in the late 1960s, Princess Sophie was the mother of five older children (from her first marriage to Prince Christoph), and married to Prince George of Hanover, with whom she had three more children, two boys, Welf and Georg, and a girl, Friederike. They spent their time between Germany and Greece. Her two younger teenagers, Georg and Friederike (who was called "Filly"), became friends of our children.

Because their ages were the same, our kids enjoyed waterskiing and dancing at the Corcyra Beach Hotel, together with other Greek friends, and we would often take turns pulling the entire family on skis behind our small motorboat. After Corfu's severe storm in 1970 – the year we met Admiral Yates – it was Princess Sophie who sounded the alarm about our boat sinking at our jetty, and notified us with enough time to save it. I have many fond memories of her, and of the time we spent together on Corfu in our early years there. I especially remember the day she surprised me at lunch with a delicious vegetarian stew she had made herself. In those years, we were unaware of the more intricate details of Princess Sophie's background, other than that she was related to the British and Greek royal families. The fact that she later admitted to being a Buddhist – as well as a vegetarian – made her all the more interesting.

While we all enjoyed each other's company and had a number of similar interests – Prince George had been a member of the International Olympic Committee/ IOC, and I was preparing for my upcoming Folklore Festival in Munich, so we had much to talk about – we were also aware that the political winds in Greece were changing. The presence of police became more visible around the island, and Greek security police suddenly began to follow Sophie and George everywhere, including to our home when they came over for a visit. Sinister-looking men would post themselves outside our entrance, waiting to escort them home. As time went on, our visits became more restricted, and we began to see less of each other on the island (though we still visited in Germany). The political scene in Greece was shifting rapidly, and the country was beginning to experience a new type of political turmoil that would have a direct effect, not only on its citizens, but also on its monarchy: the Greek Military Junta.

In 1967, just after we had bought our piece of land on Corfu, Greece suddenly awoke to a military coup, initiated by a group of right-wing army officers, and the beginning of a

Tanks are ordered into the streets of Athens following a military coup in
1967 led by a group of right-wing army officers known as 'The Junta'

King Constantine of Greece with the new regime's colonels
in the early stages of the coup. He is forced into exile
and the Greek monarchy is abolished.

Protests in Athens against the
king's failure to take a firmer
stand against the new regime

totalitarian dictatorship that would last for seven years. Known by various names – the "Regime of the Colonels," the "Dictatorship," "The Generals' Coup," "The Greek Military Junta," "The Junta" – it arose out of decades of political infighting and instability between right and left political factions dating back to Greece's Civil War after the country was liberated in 1944. More recently, an increased demand for power by King Constantine II, Greece's young monarch (and nephew of Princess Sophie and Prince George,) had accelerated the crisis.

With the approval of the Johnson Administration in the United States, which, along with Junta members feared a Communist win in the upcoming scheduled elections, armored tanks suddenly entered the capital of Athens on April 17, 1967, surprising its residents, and took over the streets of the city. Within 24 hours, all of Greece was in the hands of the Junta, all leading politicians were arrested (including well-known centrists Georgios Papandreou and his son Andreas), the articles of the Greek constitution were suspended, and freedom of the press and almost all forms of civil liberties were suppressed.

Troops also surrounded King Constantine's villa in Athens. Resisting at first, the monarch eventually gave in to the new government, and though he subsequently attempted a weak counter-coup, he would be widely criticized for his initial acceptance of the colonels and forced to abdicate. Banishment of the Greek royal family soon followed, along with a complete abolishment of the monarchy in Greece in 1973.

Constantine and his family went into exile in Rome and London for more than 40 years, and only recently returned to live in Athens in 2013.

The Coup also affected the Greek islands, including Corfu, though we, as foreigners, did not feel as much of the immediate impact as our Greek friends. We did notice, though, that our Greek gardener, Costas, suddenly appeared without his usual beard (beards were now banned by the Colonels, except on priests). When we visited one of our local restaurants known for its bouzouki music and souvlaki, tourists were no longer allowed to engage in that venerable Greek tradition of smashing plates – much to their dismay. Anti-communist posters extolling the new government as "saviors against anarchy" began appearing all over town, and flying the Greek flag in front of homes and businesses owned by Greek citizens became an obligation. As a result of these political tensions, Oscar and I seriously reconsidered our plans to complete our house on the island (we had already purchased the land and started construction), but because of the financial and legal commitments already in play, it was too late to back out.

In the meantime, Georgios Papadopoulos was appointed Prime Minister and, armed with the battle-cry of a "communist conspiracy" in Greece, the Junta began a purge that reached into all aspects of its society, including the press, the military, the government, its legal system, and academia. Surveillance on the daily lives of citizens (not unlike that of the eastern-block Communist countries) became the norm – even during social activities, as we had experienced with Princess Sophie's visits to our house. Years later, we would learn that thousands of people had been imprisoned, exiled to remote Greek islands, or tortured.

Under the Junta, while there was also strong censorship of Greek art, film, literature, and music (Costa-Gavras' film "Z" and Mikis Theodorakis' music were forbidden), Western music and rock groups and hippie colonies living on some of the Greek islands were not affected, as long as they stayed out of trouble. Eager to develop tourism on the islands (Mykonos and Corfu, for example), the Greek government didn't view them as a threat.

During this time (1967-1972), Greece also experienced a strong economic boom, fueled by pro-business incentives, low-unemployment, public spending, construction, and foreign investment – particularly in its tourist industry. As a result, Corfu went through the rapid transformation of a quiet historic and primarily rural community to a sophisticated tourist mecca. Paved roads began to appear all over the island – leading to more buses, cars, congestion, and noise. Investments in construction, frequently mired in financial scandals, led to larger hotels and smaller inns at strategic points of the island (often leading past our house); foreigners began buying more properties inland and along the coast; and Corfu became heavily promoted by travel agents the world over as one of the premier Greek island destinations.

As Greece's economic infrastructure was developing, so too was the opposition to the dictatorship. A number of democratic resistance groups formed both in and outside the country, and in 1968, an assassination attempt by junta resistance fighter and poet Alexandros (Alekos) Panagoulis on Papadopoulos failed. Panagoulis, regarded as a hero, would survive torture and prison, and eventually become a member of Parliament after the Junta years. He was later killed under mysterious circumstances in a car crash in 1976.

Also regarded as a hero – though perhaps as a much sadder incident – was a young

1973 protests by students of the Athens Polytechnic University against the
Greek military Junta that help topple the dictatorship in 1974

Corfiote protesting the Papadopoulos regime. In 1970, Kostas Georgakis, a handsome 22-year-old student attending university in Genoa, Italy, and receiving a stipend from the Greek government for his studies, set himself on fire to bring international awareness to the political dictatorship in Greece. Fearing protests at home, the Junta delayed the arrival of his remains in Corfu for months, but Georgakis's act would set in motion a series of events, including later student protests at the Athens Polytechnic Institute, which would eventually help topple the regime. A memorial is dedicated to him in the city of Corfu.

From 1970-74, resistance to the dictatorship would only grow as divisions within the Junta itself began to appear. Despite a few liberal reforms introduced by Papadopoulos (mostly to increase his own power), the fabric of the dictatorship began to unravel as large demonstrations occurred all over Greece, supported by organizations and celebrities such as actress Melina Mercouri and composer Mikis Theodorakis, who were living outside the country. Other protests ensued, including a mutiny by Greek navy commander, Nikolaos Pappas, who refused to return his ship, Velos, to Greece after completing NATO exercises in Italy. This was followed by a student uprising at the Athens Polytechnic Institute when the head of the military police and Junta hardliner, Dimitrios Ioannidis, decided to instigate his own coup, killing a number of students with a tank that he rammed through the university gates. He would set up a brief new Junta in Greece in 1974, and then bring about a coup on the island of Cyprus that would overthrow the president of Cyprus, Archbishop Makarios II, and draw Turkey into a war.

The dictatorship would finally come to an end in 1974 when senior military officers withdrew their support for Ioannidis after the Cyprus invasion, and former Prime Minister Constantine Karamanlis agreed to return to Greece with his New Democracy party. He would be elected Prime Minister from 1974 to 1980, and be witness to Greece's first democratic parliament in 10 years. In 1975, all of the Junta members were convicted of high treason and death, which Karamanlis later commuted to life imprisonment. In 1999, President Clinton apologized for the involvement of the United States in its support of the coup and dictatorship.

We, however, would never see our friends, Princess Sophie and Prince George, on Corfu again, though we continued to spend all our summers, except for one: the year of the International Folklore Festival at the 1972 Olympic Games, during which time I rented the property to Nana Mouskouri, the famous Greek singer who, with sales of more than 300 million records in 13 languages worldwide, is one of the most successful female recording artists of all time.

We remained on the island for 25 years, but, after Oscar's death in 1993, I would eventually sell our summer home to a Swiss family. Years later, I returned to Corfu for one last visit.

Our Corfu summer home, Villa Serenísima,
shortly before we left the island

8. Berlin

With the encouraging reviews from the German media in 1972, my company's reputation was thriving, and we were now well-established in Germany. So it seemed to be an auspicious time to ride the positive wave of publicity. Under the heading of Eva Maze Presents, I decided to further expand International Artists Productions and my role of impresario in Europe and, for the next 20 years, would continue to compile a substantial list of quality programs for the German public and other European audiences.

The companies and artists I chose were drawn from a cross-section of the performing arts: ballet, contemporary and modern dance, folk dance, European cabaret singers, jazz vocal ensembles, classical soloists and orchestras, theatrical readings, solo performances, and classical and contemporary theater. I also realized that, with the dozens of productions in the works (which, over a span of 40 years, ended up being more than 100), I needed to increase my staff.

Working out of a large office on the lower level of our house in Berlin, I hired two people: a secretary, for the daily office work of phone calling, scheduling, typing etc., and an assistant, who, with some training, would eventually take over some of my touring responsibilities.

Berlin's famous avenue downtown, the Kurfürstendamm,
and the Kaiser Wilhelm Memorial Church in 1972

The person I chose for the latter was a gifted young actor by the name of Manfred Greve, who, years later, would become a successful German theatrical producer/ impresario in his own right. When Manfred signed on with me, he was an actor with Berlin's Schiller Theater. He had also been the German narrator for the Kabuki production I toured in Germany prior to the Olympic Games. He joined my office as coordinator of a new program of theatrical plays I decided to establish called "Theater auf Tournee" (Theater on Tour). Its logo became a theatrical mask on wheels.

In the beginning, the primary purpose of this new branch of my company was to present classical and contemporary plays that had been translated into German. Manfred would tour these plays in Germany under the Theater auf Tournee heading, while I continued to handle the international companies under International Artists Productions. In time, both programs would eventually merge under Eva Maze Presents: International Artist Productions/ Theater auf Tournee.

For Theater auf Tournee, Manfred's job was to find theaters throughout West Germany that would be interested in acquiring and presenting a selection of plays – both dramas and comedies – within a given theatrical season. We would choose the individual plays, and then

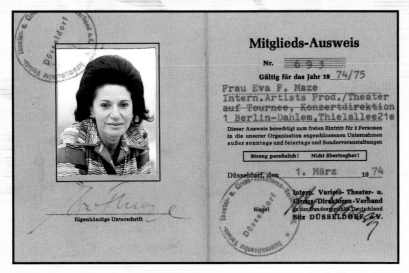

My official identification card as an established member of the Theater
Management Directors Association in Germany, and my assistant, Manfred Greve (right)

put a package together that he could sell under my name to as many municipal theaters as possible in Germany. Performance schedules were seasonal, running from the fall of a specific year through the spring of the following year. Some of the same plays were repeated season to season (depending on the success of a previous season), while others changed year to year.

The Theater auf Tournee productions were drawn from a variety of sources: Some were of German origin, while others were foreign. Most of the plays we presented were in the public domain – mainly those by Shakespeare, Ibsen, Beckett, Sophocles, Aristophanes – in which case paying for production rights was not an issue. A payment for rights was required, however, for the newer and more contemporary productions we decided to tour. In these cases, the agreements with the rights' holders were structured either on a royalty basis with a percentage off box office sales, or as a flat fee per performance paid up front. The goal was to have these traveling theatrical productions – most of which were already translated from other languages into German (though some were also performed in their original language) – appear in as many of the subsidized theaters (large and small) in Germany as possible, and for Manfred to oversee this program while I continued to tour with my other companies. At the time, there were about 2,000 such theaters in Germany.

Program brochure for the 1979/80 season, with Burt Bacharach's musical *Promises, Promises (Das Appartement)*; Max Frisch's play, *The Arsonists (Biedermann und die Brandstifter)*; the Zurich Opera Ballet; Antonio Gades' Spanish National Ballet; and the Bella Lewitzky Dance Company

Program brochure for the 1980/81 season, with Henrik Ibsen's play, *John Gabriel Borkman*; Conductor Willi Boskovsky and the Vienna Johann Strauss Orchestra; London's Ballet Rambert; the Swiss mime group, Mummenschanz; and an evening of song and dance called *Broadway Showtime*

Once we established our playlist for the season, we would obtain a non-binding, signed commitment of availability from the lead actors or an entire company, for a particular play and specific dates (secondary actors would be selected once the engagement with the theater was confirmed). A final agreement with them would only be signed once the theatrical venue was confirmed by contract.

A revised annual brochure, listing all the productions for the upcoming season and availability for a specific period of time during that season, was sent out a year in advance to the 2,000 or so theatres and concert halls in cities and towns across West Germany. If there was interest in a particular play, the theatrical manager would buy the production – usually for a one-night performance – and sign a final contract with me. Manfred and I would then hire a German director for the play and work out its final performance schedule for the season.

At first, a four-month fall or spring season included three to five plays, each to be performed at approximately 30 venues, with one or two evening engagements at every location. As Theater auf Tournee became better known, we added other productions to its program (including some of my foreign companies), so that the number of groups or artists on tour grew to as many as ten in a given season. The distances from venue to venue were short, and the cast, costumes, and scenic designs were usually transported during the day by bus. Each theater would provide its own lighting technicians.

A typical day involved traveling to a venue in the morning, setting up and rehearsing in the early afternoon after a brief rest, and performing in the evening. This type of schedule was often grueling, though the actors seemed to adjust better to it than, for example, dancers, who began touring under Theater auf Tournee as well. Because of the additional time required by dance companies for physical warm-ups and rehearsals, the tight touring schedule was met, at times, with resistance, as with the Alvin Ailey Dance Theater and Lar Lubovitch Dance Company.

In situations where the rights to a play were acquired through a signed contract with the rights' owners (in Germany, these were typically publishing houses, specializing in dramatic and musical works), and the production was cancelled by the theater prior to my signing the contract with the venue (which happened very rarely in the 20 years Theater auf Tournee was in existence), we were required to pay a penalty to the publishing house. This was a professional risk I had to assume on my part. However, at no time during these 20 years did any of the Ger-

Program brochure for the 1984/85 season, with Shakespeare's *Twelfth Night (Was Ihr Wollt)*; the Finnish National Ballet; Tahiti's Grand Ballet "Iaora Tahiti"; Italy's I Colombaioni pantomime group; and a cabaret show with German actress Uta Sax, *Frauen, Hexen und Vampire (Women, Witches and Vampires)*

Program brochure for the 1986/87 season, with Chekhov's *Uncle Vanya (Onkel Wanya)*, New York's Lar Lubovitch Dance Company; France's Théâtre Chorégraphique de Rennes; and Britain's Natural Theatre Company from Bath, two comedies, *Scarlatti's Birthday Party* and *Her Majesty's Pleasure*

151

On tour through Germany for four successful seasons with three musicals by England's Natural Theatre Company, a well-known street theater company from Bath. They featured the satirical comedies of *Scarlatti's Birthday Party*, *Scarlatti's Wedding*, *Spy Society* and *Her Majesty's Pleasure* (a spoof about Queen Victoria).

man theaters renege on their agreement with us once the contract for a specific engagement was signed with them. If, for any reason, an actor had to drop out of the production, the role was recast, and the actor was not penalized.

As soon as a play was set to go, and the director and lead actors were on board, we would hire the set and costume designers, along with the secondary actors. Many of the plays I produced were well-known classic masterpieces: *The Diary of Anne Frank (Das Tagebuch der Anne Frank)* by Anne Frank Huis, *The Mad Woman of Chaillot (Die Irre von Chaillot)* by Jean Giraudoux, *John Gabriel Borkman* by Henrik Ibsen, *An Ideal Husband (Ein Idealer Gatte)* by Oscar Wilde, *The Wedding (Die Heirat)* by Nikolai Gogol, *The Little Foxes (Die Kleinen Füchse)* by Lillian Hellman,

Twelfth Night (Was Ihr Wollt), and *Comedy of Errors (Komödie der Irrungen)* by William Shakespeare, to name a few. There were also several Greek dramas that were performed in ancient Greek, including Aristophanes' *Peace (Frieden)* and Sophocles' *Oedipus Rex (Ödipus Rex)*. In 1987, *Uncle Vanya (Onkel Wanya)*, Anton Chekhov's tale of unrequited love, would be the last of the classical plays we produced.

Our list also consisted of several musicals: *No, No Nannette (Tea for Two)* by Vincent Youmans, *A Slice of Saturday Night*, London's award-winning musical about the iconic dreams of love, peace, and flower power of the 1960s – both performed in German – and four musical comedies presented in English by Britain's Natural Theatre in the late 1980s/early 1990s: *Spy Society, Scarlatti's Birthday Party, Scarlatti's Wedding*, and *Her Majesty's Pleasure*.

There were some wonderful German directors in those days who worked with us. They included the award-winning Oswald Döpke of German ZDF Television, who staged Chekhov's *Onkel Wanya (Uncle Vanya)*, Hans Korte, who directed Ibsen's *John Gabriel Borkman*, and Harry Buckwitz who, among others, had also been the General Manager of the Frankfurt Oper in my early years in the city. When I met with him to discuss our terms for directing *The Arsonists (Biedermann und die Brandstifter)*, a controversial play about fate and identity by Swiss playwright Max Frisch, I reminded him of the time when the roles were reversed and he had engaged me for the short character dance part in the *Sleeping Beauty* ballet. As we sat over lunch discussing the Frisch play, I couldn't help but tease him about the fact that I was paying him much more to direct the play than I had been paid for my ten performances as the queen-mother in the ballet. In fact, my performance fee for the ballet at the time had been so low, my husband suggested I donate it to a good cause. As with the compensation issue years earlier in London, I again felt that I had earned it, deciding instead to collect my payment in one lump sum at the end of my run so that the amount seemed larger. It was, however, only a fraction of the 12,000 DM (German Marks) I paid Harry Buckwitz for his work, but it was well worth it: *The Arsonists* was performed 120 times during our 1979-80 season.

I also had the pleasure of working with some very talented set designers – in particular Christian Jenssen, who created the set and props for *The Arsonists (Biedermann und die Brandstifter)*, and would go on to collaborate with me on a number of plays. To this day, Christian still remains in touch, sending me, as a New Year's gift each year, one of his lovely, original drawings.

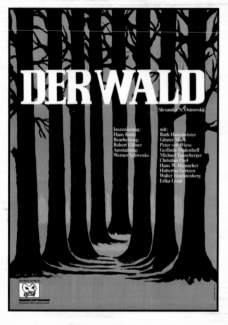

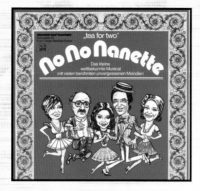

Plays performed in German under our *Theater auf Tournee* program included (p.154, in order, left to right): Shakespeare's *Twelfth Night*, Ibsen's *John Gabriel Borkman*, Chekhov's *Uncle Vanya*, Giraudoux's *The Mad Woman of Chaillot*, Ostrowsky's *The Forest*, Sternheim's *The Trousers*, Gogol's *Marriage*, Frisch's *The Arsonists*, Sophocles' *Oedipus Rex*, and Sternheim's *1913*. Musicals included (above, in order shown, left to right): Youmans' *No No Nanette*, an evening of show tunes, *Broadway Showtime*, Benatzky's *My Sister and I*, Simon and Bacharach's *Promises Promises*, and a German variety show, *Black Market*.

The German production of *Diary of Anne Frank* by
Frances Goodrich and Albert Hackett that toured with
much success throughout Germany in 1976 and 1977
under our auspices as a co-venture with the Hamburger
Kammerspiele Theater. The play was also broadcast
live on German television.

Off-stage, these productions were not
without their dramatic and, at times, amusing
mishaps. On one occasion – in *The Diary of Anne
Frank (Das Tagebuch der Anne Frank)* – the German
actress Marina Reid, who played the role of
Peter van Daan's mother (of the second family
hiding in the attic with the Franks) accidentally
fell and broke her nose backstage during the
show, causing much concern about her health,
and whether she could finish the program.
There were no understudies and we considered
shutting the play down for the evening, but
after several bags of ice were applied to her face
between acts, she bravely performed to the end
of the show – despite her intense pain. She was
a real trouper!

Then again in this same drama, Edith
Frank, Anne's mother, played by the actress Herta
Kravina, barely made it to the bus one morning
as it was leaving with the cast for the next venue,
arriving disheveled and flustered because she
had lost her bedroom slippers in the hotel where
they were staying. The sight of her complaining
as she made her entrance into the bus with her
wig on lopsided, prompted the actors waiting for
her on board to burst out laughing.

In one instance during the tour of this
play, a member of the cast had actually been
left behind when he overslept and missed the
departure of the bus following a night of heavy

drinking by the hotel pool. After fifteen minutes on the road, we realized he was missing and had to turn back to pick him up (I was traveling with the cast at the time).

As the success of Theater auf Tournee grew and took on its own identity with the German plays, so did the other programs under International Artists Productions. While they were well received by the German media, it was important to me personally that they also be engaging, thought-provoking, and unique – as per the original mission and criteria of my company – and I liked the fact that they were so varied.

There were evenings of chansons, ballads, and cabaret with famous European artists such as Milva, a highly polished and professional chanteuse with a magnificent voice, known for her one-woman shows of boulevard songs; Catherine Gayer, an American soprano with the Berlin Opera, who received rave reviews for her renditions of Kurt Weill and George Gerschwin songs, Broadway tunes, and German boulevard ditties of the 1900s with a program she called *Kabarett für Feinschmecker* (Cabaret for the Discriminating Public); the Austrian singer, Elfriede Ott, famous in Germany for her Viennese songs; and Uta Sax, a German actress and singer, who had written a one-woman show based on witches and vampires called *Frauen, Hexen, und Vampire (Women, Witches, and Vampires)*.

Von Frauen, Hexen und Vampiren

Lieder, Texte und Chansons vom Mittelalter bis heute

von und mit

Uta Sax

am Flügel Curt Gold
Künstlerische Leitung
Jean-Pierre Liégeois

Eva Maze presents

theater auf tournee
international artists productions berlin

Well-known German stage actress Uta Sax, performing in a one-woman cabaret show created by her, called *Von Frauen, Hexen und Vampiren (Of Women, Witches and Vampires)*, with songs and texts dating back to the Middle Ages

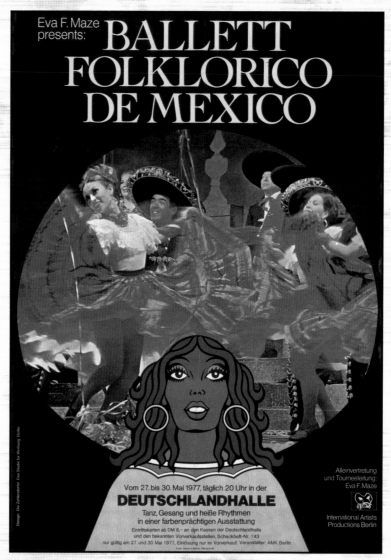

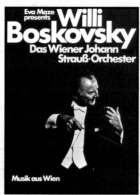

Foreign companies (dance, orchestra, folklore) presented under International Artists Productions / Theater Auf Tournee included Ballet Folklórico de México, and (left/ top to bottom): The Finnish National Ballet, Miyagi Minoru's Dance Troupe, Ballet Rambert, and the Vienna Johann Strauss Orchestra under Willi Boskovsky.

Other international companies that toured under our logo from 1972 to 1992 also featured pantomime artists Colombaioni, as well as (right/ top to bottom): The José Limon Dance Company, clowns Mini and Maxi, Lar Lubovitch Dance Company, and Ballet Théatre Joseph Russillo from France.

159

Popular Italian singer Milva on tour with us through Germany in 1975, with renditions of dramatic cabaret songs by Kurt Weill and Bertolt Brecht

Cabaret acts had long been popular in Germany. Milva, in particular, sold out to theaters everywhere. An Italian fisherman's daughter who couldn't read music, she captivated audiences with her powerful cabaret voice and flaming red hair (she was known in Italy as "La Rossa"– the red-headed). Wrapped on stage in a boa, and perched on a chair under a single beam of light, she delivered dramatic renditions of Berthold Brecht, Kurt Weill, Edith Piaf, and the Austrian composer, Hanns Eisler. She was methodical and precise, and very particular about lighting with the technicians. Popular in Germany in the 1970s, she had a lot of style and sophistication, was very organized, and her dressing room was immaculate. Needless to say, we got along very well, and the audiences were eager to see her.

Germany – and Europe in general – has always had a deep love for culture (of all types) that goes back hundreds of years. After starting out as the exclusive domain of the courts and nobility, the performing arts gradually expanded to the middle and working classes, and culture became imbedded into the social fabric of Europe.

Under the Nazi regime, the public was given limited access to foreign plays and modern concepts, so that by the 1960s and 1970s, people were hungry for information and eager to catch up on cultural programs that had eluded them. Once their daily needs were met (food, shelter, education, etc.), whatever was left over financially in their household budgets was directed toward filling this void, and top priorities became discovering new trends and paying for cultural programs they had missed, or had previously been verboten.

In fact, after World War II, all the western European countries – long known for their tradition of celebrating writers and composers – expanded their citizens' access to culture. With monies levied from personal taxes, they developed social institutions and public policies that supported culture and arts endowments. This led to generous subsidies of the arts, in particular for museums and the performing arts, and opened up a person's accessibility to them – both physically and financially. In Germany, theaters were built in every corner of the country, and state-subsidized cultural programs kept ticket prices reasonable. As a result, the public became very receptive to new ideas in the performing arts and other art forms – fostering a trend that has continued to this day.

Keenly aware of the innate intellectual and cultural curiosity of the Germans (and Europeans in general), their appreciation for innovative ideas, and my own identity with Europe, it was not difficult for me to gauge the public's preferences and what would work for them. My selections were high quality, whether they came from the classical or contemporary arenas of dance, symphonic orchestras, vocal groups, musicals, mime, solo readings of texts (for the more intellectual crowd), cabaret or just an evening of chansons.

Selecting the international productions always followed a similar methodology: I would hear or read about different artists or companies from a variety of sources, consider referrals or recommendations by others, and check out the specific artist or group in person. After attending one of its performances, I would evaluate its quality and uniqueness, and if I thought it would do well in Germany and/or elsewhere in Europe, would invite the company to tour with us under a guaranteed contract based on the number of venues and performances. Again, a final contract would only be drawn up after the tour schedule was confirmed with the theater managers. I would then travel with each company for at least one night's performance.

As with the German theatrical performances, the Theater of Tournee schedule for the international artists usually featured one-night appearances at each location, though, in some cases, there were more. At the end of each performance, I collected payment (usually in cash) from the administrative office of the theater, and we would both keep careful financial statements

World-renowned Swiss pantomime group, Mummenschanz – famous for its surrealistic props, masks, and toilet
paper rolls – toured with International Artists Productions in Europe after a 3-year run on Broadway

for tax purposes. Nightly performance rates in those days for the types of productions I handled ranged from DM 4,000 for the lesser-known companies to DM 12,000 per evening for the more prominent ones. Most fell somewhere in between – regardless of whether they were German plays or foreign companies. The artists or companies were paid out of this revenue, as per our contractual agreement.

International companies that participated in this intensive touring program from the 1970s through the 1980s ran the gamut of unique, relatively unknowns such the Miyagi Minoru Okinawa Dance Troupe of Japan, Grand Ballet de Tahiti, Iora Tahiti, and Italian Colombaioni pantomime group, to the more established contemporary Bella Lewitzky and Joyce Trisler dance companies, Ballet Rambert London, Harkness Ballet of New York City, Swedish Cullberg Ballet (with its edgy choreography), Antonio Gades Baile Español, Zurich Opera Ballet, Finnish National Ballet, Lar Lubovitch Dance Company, and Wiener Johann Strauss Orchestra under Willi Boskovsky.

We were also fortunate to present under our auspices the very popular and exciting Swiss Mummenschanz, troupe – known for its pioneering routines with toilet paper, colorful abstract shapes, and masks – in Germany, Lichtenstein, and Switzerland, where they dazzled sold-out audiences, and were in such high demand – especially in Berlin at the Akademie der Künste – that extra security personnel was brought in to lock the doors to the theater in front of long lines of people clamouring for tickets.

While some companies were booked for weeks under the Theater auf Tournee program, others performed for only a few evenings at a time. The American Ballet Theatre (ABT), which was co-sponsored with the Münchner Staatstheater (State Theater of Munich) at the Munich Olympiapark was one such example. ABT had accepted our invitation to perform in Munich for two nights. Mikhail Baryshnikov had recently defected from the U.S.S.R. and become a big sensation with the company. Those two evenings under our auspices in Munich, July 1977, the company – which then included ballet greats Gelsey Kirkland, Eric Bruhn, Ivan Nagy, Cynthia Gregory, Martine van Hamel, Marianna Tcherkassky, and John Prinz – performed to thunderous applause. They included a wonderful program of Alvin Ailey's *The River*, the Pas-de-deux from *Don Quixote*, José Limón's *The Moor's Pavane*, and Twyla Tharp's *Push Comes to Shove*. On the second night, Mikhail Baryshnikov and Gelsey Kirkland danced the complete classical ballet *Giselle*, which brought down the house.

The ABT had actually arrived in Germany without musicians and was looking for an orchestra to tour with them through Europe, including the two nights in Munich. I was aware that the conductor of Romania's premier Bucharest Philharmonic Orchestra, Mihai Brediceanu – with whom I had worked before – was touring with his orchestra in Belgium at the time. So I invited him to come to Munich and play with the American Ballet Theatre, which he accepted, but only after receiving authorization from the Romanian government (in 1976, Romania was still under control of the Soviet Union). While Romanian security was present, though not obvious, the pairing of a ballet company featuring a high-profile recent defector from the Soviet Union with an orchestra from a Soviet satellite country proved to be an interesting situation that was not lost on the press. The match worked out so well that the Bucharest Philharmonic ended up traveling to Paris with the American Ballet Theatre for additional performances, albeit under another pre-arranged management agency.

After the *Giselle* performance, I invited Misha (Baryshnikov) out to dinner. He had expressed a desire for Chinese food and I obliged. He was about 28 at the time, handsome, very pleasant, and had a good sense of humor. He was especially happy to have danced in *Push Comes to*

Münchner Olympiapark GmbH und Eva F. Maze present:

AMERICAN BALLET THEATRE

mit Mikhail Baryshnikov
Die Bukarester Philharmoniker

Montag/Dienstag
11./12. Juli 1977
jeweils 20.30 Uhr

OLYMPIAHALLE

Karten ab 20,—DM am Eissportstadion im Olympiapark (3864-877) und bei den bekannten Vorverkaufsstellen

The American Ballet Theatre performs for two sold-out evenings at the Olympiahalle Stadium, which seats more than 12,000 people. One of the highlights of the evening was the ballet *Giselle* (top), starring Mikhail Baryshnikov and Gelsey Kirkland.

Shove, perhaps already foreshadowing his future endeavors in the modern dance world. He had defected from Russia's Kirov Ballet while on tour in Canada three years earlier and, along with his position as principal dancer with ABT, was also guest-dancing with the New York City Ballet under George Balanchine, and London's Royal Ballet. Known as one of the best male dancers of all time (Nijinsky and Nureyev, among others), he would go on to receive numerous awards, become the Artistic Director of the American Ballet Theatre, found the White Oak Dance Project with Mark Morris, perform in television and cinema, and more recently, establish the Baryshnikov Arts Center in New York, now a magnet for innovative artists from the art worlds of music, dance, theater, and multi-media.

On my list of highly talented artists who also toured with me for a number of years – and with whom I would forge a long friendship – was a unique vocal group known as the Swingle Singers, that had burst onto the scene in 1962 to high acclaim in France. I had originally seen – or more precisely heard them sing – during a trip to Paris, and knew at once they would be a hit in Germany. A very professional group of eight extremely talented international singers representing different voice ranges, it included two sopranos, led by Christiane Legrand (sister of composer Michel Legrand), two altos, two tenors, and two bases. Using their voices as musical instruments, the Swingle Singers ensemble became known for singing classical music a capella with jazz and scat improvisations.

The original Swingle Singers had been formed in Paris by a classically-trained American pianist from Mobile, Alabama, Ward Swingle, out of a group of former back-up vocalists to the famous French singers, Charles Aznavour and Edith Piaf. A music prodigy who mastered a number of instruments, Swingle had already performed with several big bands as a high-school student and loved "scatting," a vocal form of singing without words, usually associated with jazz and made popular by Ella Fitzgerald. He had graduated with honors from the Cincinnati Conservatory of Music, studied with the famous pianist Walter Gieseking, and was living in Europe, married to a French musician, Françoise Demorest. Ward Swingle would go on to create a groundbreaking a capella sound by taking scat and applying it vocally to the works of famous classical composers, including Bach, Mozart, Vivaldi, and Beethoven, among others.

By the time I first met them in the late 1960s, the Swingle Singers were already popular. Starting out as an informal scat group that recorded sessions of Bach's *Well-Tempered Clavier* primarily for friends, they had risen to fame after radio stations began playing

On tour through Europe with the talented and sophisticated a cappella scat group, Swingle Singers, founded by Ward Swingle (top photo, to my right). They perform a program of Bach and Mozart in cocktail attire (bottom).

segments of their first album, *Jazz Sebastian Bach*, which earned the first of five Grammy awards for their various recordings. Their renditions of Bach's Fugue in G Minor, Mozart's "A Little Night Music," and Beethoven's "Clair de Lune" became instant hits.

The original French group would then disband in 1973 and be replaced by a second successful Swingle Singers company in London that continues to this day. I personally kept in touch with Ward Swingle for many years, and was very sad to learn that this very gifted and kind man had died in 2015, at the age of 87.

Traveling on tour with such highly talented and professional artists will almost always produce moments of anxiety behind the scenes, and being on the road with the Swingle Singers was no exception. At one of our Frankfurt concerts, we got caught up in an amusing situation when the group arrived at the theater without Ward Swingle's tuxedo and shoes. The singers always wore formal attire on stage, but Ward's luggage had been lost. Once again, my very reliable husband, Oscar, came to our rescue, loaning Ward his own tuxedo and a pair of shoes, until the piece of luggage finally turned up (it was a miracle they were the same size!).

When he was not working at Templehof Airport, Oscar would always be in the wings during one performance or another, ready to step in when problems arose – as unexpected situations and mishaps regularly surfaced in these types of events. I will always be grateful to him for that.

As my success grew in the 20 years that followed the 1972 Olympic Games in Munich, Pan Am, on the other hand, was gradually falling apart....

Throughout my 40 years as an impresario, Oscar had continued to work in Pan Am's flight operations in Asia and Europe, and had seen the company blossom from a tiny Caribbean mail carrier to a global enterprise that became the standard bearer for commercial aviation. This would unfortunately not last, and after a long period of profitable growth with its routes and fleets – as well as its stellar reputation – the company's success took a downturn in the early 1970s and began to suffer serious financial losses over the next 20 years.

With intense competition from other airlines, a worsening of economic conditions (rising fuel costs and the 1973 oil crisis), the expensive maintenance of older fleets, unsupportive federal policies (Pan Am was deemed an international carrier and not allowed to operate in the U.S.), and a series of poor management decisions by a succession of CEOs (such as the purchase of National Airlines and the Airbus), Pan Am was threatened repeatedly with bankruptcy. To remain afloat, it was gradually forced to sell its routes (its Pacific and London routes went to United Airlines), as well as its assets (the Pan Am Building and InterContinental Hotels, among others). This was further complicated by a failed attempt to acquire Northwest Airlines in 1989, which would have helped consolidate its presence in the United States, as well as the 1988 Lockerbie, Scotland, terrorist disaster of Flight 103 and ensuing lawsuits (Oscar and I were actually scheduled to be on this flight from Frankfurt to New York, but were offloaded in the last minute because of space availability).

So after more than 70 years, this iconic airline became a shadow of its former self, and was forced to declare bankruptcy on January 8, 1991. Despite an attempt to revive Pan Am in 1991, the tattered pieces that remained were eventually absorbed by Delta Airlines on December 4, 1991.

When Delta Airlines took over what was left of Pan Am, Oscar accepted an opportunity to continue on with them. My husband had witnessed firsthand the growth of an industry that had begun with mail carriers and flying boats, and revolutionized transportation globally with jumbo jets that could cross the world in less than 24 hours. Half a century later, aviation was still in his blood. Though plagued by high blood pressure and cholesterol, he was not ready to retire. At the same time, everything in the aviation business was changing, and the era of computerization was in full swing. Delta Airlines required that everyone be recertified and up-to-date with the most recent computer training, and I remember how Oscar, who was now in his early 70s, came home excited and amazed at Delta's high-tech campus atmosphere in Atlanta, but also exhausted after the intense training he had received there. He would work for Delta Airlines for only a few months after Pan Am's downfall. Shortly after his transfer, Oscar collapsed as a result of a massive cerebral hemorrhage, and sadly pass away at the age of 74. And I lost my most devoted ally and companion.

For me, the timing of Oscar's death couldn't have been more painful or symbolic. He had been my "Rock of Gibraltar," always at my side, and though we had our problems – like any married couple – I couldn't envision life without him. While I was mourning him personally, I was also mourning the end of a brilliant era, which we had had the privilege of enjoying in so many beneficial ways together. Because of Oscar's long association with Pan Am, our family had been given the luxury of front-row seating to the cultures of the world, and I and our children reaped enormous benefits from it. Oscar was highly respected in his field – even called a 'legend' by some. When I made the necessary arrangements to bring him back to the burial plot we had chosen together at Princeton Cemetery in New Jersey, five ex-Pan Am pilots, who had worked with Oscar for many years at Pan Am, but now were flying for Delta, attended the funeral service in their Pan Am uniforms as a show of respect for him. As the casket was lowered into the ground, they saluted him in the same way captains were saluted as they entered the airplanes of times past, and I was deeply moved by their tribute.

Remnants pieced together of Pan Am Flight 103's explosion
over Lockerbie, Scotland, in 1988

9. Paris

I had grown up knowing that Bucharest, the city of my birth, was called the Paris of the Balkans. In fact, Romanians very much admired and identified with French culture, and it was emulated throughout the country, particularly in its architecture, education, and fashion. Bucharest's wide tree-lined avenues were similar to the boulevards of Paris, and even today, its city center retains much of the French flavor of the late 19th and early 20th centuries – despite years of massive construction under the Communist regime. The French baroque style still adorns old palaces that have been turned into other types of buildings, such as the Enesco Museum, formerly known as the Cantacuzino Palace, and the CEC bank building, designed in 1900 by a French architect, that now serves as the headquarters of Romania's national savings bank.

French was also Romania's second language and many Romanians were educated in France. The liceu (middle and secondary school) system was actually modeled after that of the French lycée.

French fashion of the 1920s and 1930s permeated daily life as well, and the latest Parisian trends were forever being copied by Romanian designers and seamstresses all over the city – both in the stores and at home.

Paris at sunset with its wide avenues of (l to r) Iena, Marceau, and Champs-Elysées,
designed in the mid 1800s by Georges-Eugène Haussmann

So I had always imagined Paris to be this mysterious, special place – one that I hoped to experience for myself one day in greater depth. I didn't expect the Bucharest of my youth to be on par with the grandeur of Paris – with its splendid museums, old palaces, elegant architecture, and everything that makes the French capital such an extraordinary and romantic city. Yet, from the time my parents and I had breezed through the City of Lights on our way to the United States from Bucharest, I had always wanted to return to this city as a resident. Those few enchanting moments as a young teen walking down Montmartre and the Champs-Elysées with my Romanian friends in 1939 – and the brief professional trips that followed – had only served to reinforce an unshakable notion that living in Paris some day would just be fabulous. By immersing myself daily in the French culture, I knew that I would not only realize one of my childhood dreams, I would also be able to develop and thrive both personally and intellectually.

The city's sophistication and bustling worlds of art, food, and fashion were very much in tune with where I was at the moment. In his book, *A Moveable Feast*, Ernest Hemingway had once written, "If you are lucky enough to have lived in Paris as a young man, then wherever you go for the rest of your life, it stays with you, for Paris is a moveable feast." As a woman 'of a certain age,' I couldn't agree with him more.

Of course, knowing the French language would come in handy as well. I had learned French early on in Romania, and even as a child, thought the words had an elegant timbre to them. As an adult, I spoke it with ease, and whenever I visited the city for business or pleasure, never had a problem communicating with the French people or assimilating into their culture. Perhaps it helped that I already spoke a number of languages, or that I just had a talent for them, but being able to communicate in French rather fluently would definitely be an asset in making me feel at home in the French capital.

In 1993, Oscar, who had always had my back both emotionally and financially, was no longer by my side. When I thought about our relationship, it often reminded me of the shape of an airplane: I had been the propeller, forever pushing forward in search of new adventures, while he remained the steady and strong fuselage, always supporting me in my endeavors. Every once in while, the engine would sputter (professionally or personally), but when times got tough, he was always there to say that I had a choice to walk away from any unpleasant situation. Though we had our differences, we made a good team, and after he died, part me of just shut down. At the age of 70, I was emotionally and physically exhausted. Oscar's passing – compounded by the fact that I had driven myself so much over the years – made me realize just how much I needed some rest and a change of scenery. And, as I found myself more often than not alone (my daughters were living in the Washington, DC, area, pursuing their own careers, Stephanie as a photojournalist, Lauri as a psychotherapist), living by myself in Berlin became more difficult. So, after 40 years in the theater business, I decided to hang up my hat as an impresario, close my Berlin office and International Artists Productions for good, and move to Paris to live out my fantasy of becoming *une Parisienne*. I guess I could have stayed on in Berlin, or moved elsewhere in Europe, but I had already spent more than 30 years of my life in Germany, and I yearned for a different environment. Never shy about challenges, I also thought it was the right time to experience something new.

My last two productions on tour in the early 1990s:
the musical, *A Slice of Saturday Night* (top), and
dance company, *Théâtre Chorégraphique de Rennes*

As my business was winding down in Berlin (it would take another year for it to come to a complete halt), I was still committed to two tours in 1993 – a British production from London's West End called *A Slice of Saturday Night / A New '60s Musical*, directed by Marc Urquhart, and a French contemporary dance group, Théâtre Choréographique de Rennes (my last theatrical presentation in German had been Chekhov's *Onkel Wanya* in 1987).

In the meantime, I also rented a small apartment in Paris around the corner of the Champs-Elysées, on Rue de Penthièvre in the 8th arrondissement and commuted between Berlin and Paris. As I prepared to take up permanent residence in Paris at the end of 1993, I kept my house in Berlin for another year. It was then that I also decided to sell our Greek summer home on Corfu, which had held so many cherished memories for me for close to 25 years. This would definitely be a year of transition, loss, grieving, and pain, but one that was also filled with some anticipation for what lay ahead. My husband had died, my company was coming to an end, and my beloved house on the island of Corfu, that we had named "La Serenísima" (Most Serene One), would soon be gone as well. Paris, however, was beckoning…

Having always believed that setting short- and long-term goals – both personally and professionally – were key to one's success in life, I felt I had reached mine and needed to move on. There was much to absorb at once, and my way of dealing with it was to keep busy. I also welcomed the change.

For those of us gypsies, who move from place to place, living in different countries around the world for lengthy periods of time, change can be both a blessing and a curse. A blessing, because the exposure to the vast array of cultures does help you become sensitized to the variety of human beings on this planet, and to those who are different from you. In turn, you eventually come to realize that you're just a small piece of a gigantic puzzle of interlocking parts that depend on each other for survival.

A curse, because your identity is often put into question. While many of us learn to adapt to each new place rather easily (it somehow becomes engrained in your blood), there are times when you feel you belong both everywhere and nowhere at the same time. With each new experience in a foreign culture, you imagine – if you choose to do so – becoming part of that culture, especially if you speak the language with some fluency and are able to connect with the psyche of its people. Yet, despite the daily immersion in and osmosis of the social mores and thinking of that culture, you also find yourself wondering who you are – which for some is more difficult to determine than for others. Then, too, there can be a disconnect between the way you feel personally about yourself in your new environment and the way others perceive you as a non-native. More often than not, regardless of how much you try to assimilate into your new surroundings and cultural mindset, you are likely to be seen as a foreigner, and will be treated as such. An exception to this may perhaps be in the United States, where the great melting pot has been primed (at least until now) to absorb numerous nationalities simultaneously, though at times with great resistance and effort – and across generations of assimilation.

So you live abroad for years on end, and to make up for any feeling of inadequacy, you imagine yourself a citizen of the world, each foot straddling a different continent, though at a deeper level, you often find yourself struggling with an identity crisis, forever questioning your own. The place of your birth and childhood probably stays with you for life as well (my Romanian roots have always remained strong, probably because I spent my first 16 years in Bucharest), and while the command of language really does help you connect with the other culture intellectually and emotionally, many of us still continue to struggle with where we do, in fact, belong.

Our family was American (I was a naturalized American), but in my own mind, I didn't really feel very American. I identified far more with my European roots and was a bit of a snob about that. I had come to the United states in 1939 at the young age of sixteen, when my parents and I moved in with my uncle in Chicago.

Six months later, when we settled in Brooklyn, New York, I made a point to perfect my English, in preparation for a good American education at Lincoln High School (and eventually college). Although I was happy we escaped the Nazi invasion in Europe, I didn't fit easily into American culture, not at first anyway. Having lived an elegant middle-class life in Europe (without much money), I had developed a deep appreciation for aesthetics, probably passed on to me by my mother, who had an affinity for quality and style. She made sure, for example, that I was always dressed in the latest hand-tailored fashions – as per the European customs of the time. So those aesthetics (and my love of fashion in general) had been instilled in me since childhood – as was also a common sense of courtesy toward others. When we settled in New York, I found Americans to be rather sloppy (both in lifestyle and dress), their behavior, quite rude (especially in school), their personality, somewhat dull, and their attitude toward new arrivals, whom they called 'foreigners,' not very welcoming. Though I did appreciate the freedom of expression in the United States, and the fact that kids asked many questions in class, for example, I was not used to the lack of respect – even then – that the students showed their teachers (we, as Europeans, were always taught to treat our teachers with high regard).

Neither did I like the sense of conformity that was the norm in the United States. Though I personally felt 'accepted' in high school, I was also considered 'different,' so the friends I sought out became those like me – born abroad and 'foreign.' This suited me just fine, and probably helped shape my own character for the rest of my life. I have also valued individuality in others ever since, and to those young people who feel marginalized at school or socially, I can only say, applaud your uniqueness and don't despair, for that is what will set you apart from others in life and help you achieve your goals.

In my case, a religious identity had eluded me as well: born Jewish, I was never brought up in the faith, though Oscar's family had originally been Orthodox Jewish. Always vigilant of anti-Semitic sentiment around the globe, including in the United States when we first married (and years later in Germany), we did not include religion in our daily lives, though Oscar

Avenue des Champs-Elysées during the Christmas season, leading up to the
Arc de Triomphe. It was right around the corner from my apartment.

perhaps felt more connected to being Jewish and to Israel than I. We did, however, develop a deep appreciation for the world at large and its diversity, and this was passed on to our children.

I would leave Berlin and our rented duplex for good in 1994.

The Berlin Wall had fallen in 1989 under Mikhail Gorbachev, and, after more than 25 years of political, economic, and social divide, East and West Germany were once again united, and adapting to each other, though it would take a long time for the unification process to overcome the serious economic and social problems that prevailed.

Unemployment in what used to be East Germany was rampant – in fact, twice as high as in the West, and in some regions up to 50 percent among the young. There was also a need to resolve the marked differences in current lifestyle and political beliefs, and it would take several decades more for them to reach some equilibrium.

After selling whatever I could to our Berlin neighbors and friends, I moved my remaining furniture to Paris, first to the small apartment on Rue de Penthièvre, and then into a larger, more comfortable flat I found on Avenue Gabriel in the 8th arrondissement, down the street from the Elysée Palace. The Elysée Palace has served as the official headquarters and residence of

The view from my balcony over the Rond-Point des Champs-Elysées park, with the Grand Palais (left) and the Eiffel Tower in the distance. The park, designed in 1667 by King Louis XIV's landscaper, André LeNôtre, is one of the oldest in Paris.

My 19th-century apartment building on Avenue Gabriel in the 8th Arrondissement down the block from the Elysée Presidential Palace

the President of France since 1848. Living close to the American Embassy, the Champs-Elysées, and the Place de la Concorde, I was thrilled with my new surroundings: the large salon (living room) of my apartment had beautiful views of the Eiffel Tower in the distance that led over the end of the Jardins des Tuileries (Tuileries Gardens) and the Rond Point des Champs-Elysées at the foot of Avenue des Champs-Elysées. Named as a tribute to the 18th century architect Ange-Jacques Gabriel, who designed the Place the la Concorde under King Louis XV of France, Avenue Gabriel became an elegant street of mansions, office buildings, and private homes in the early 19th century, running parallel to the Champs-Elysées and Faubourg St. Honoré between Avenue Matignon and Place de La Concorde.

Though our 19th-century building was not in the best physical shape and upkeep of common areas left much to be desired (walls were never painted by the owners during my 16-year stay there, and a tiny elevator accommodating no more than two very slender people was never replaced), I couldn't have been happier about this location. In my own apartment on the 3rd floor (in Europe, the first floor begins above the ground floor), plumbing was a problem and needed to be modernized. With a long lease in hand, I decided to update the bathroom and kitchen myself – an acceptable practice for rentals in France (with the consent of the owner, of course). Anything that couldn't fit into the two-bedroom apartment ended up underground in *la cave*, a musty dirt cellar almost 40 feet down from ground level that could only be accessed by foot after carefully treading down steep, uneven stone stairs. Supposedly free of rats and other rodents, it was there that all of my excess furniture, boxes, and mementos – collected since 1948 – would remain for 16 years until I returned to the United States for good in 2009. When my daughter, Stephanie, came to help me make my final move and sift through all my belongings, she had to wear a mask while working in the cellar, but was amazed at how well everything had been preserved, despite the moisture, dust, and smells that had accumulated there over the past several centuries.

The building housed an interesting cast of characters, but unless a specific issue needed immediate attention, there was little interaction with them. Some were actual owners such as the CEO of Heineken beer (who had other residences as well), some rented for a short time, such as Stella McCartney, the daughter of former Beatle, Paul McCartney, and American photographer, Linda McCartney, who briefly lived next door to me. At the time, McCartney was an aspiring fashion designer working as creative director for the French fashion house, Chloé (succeeding Karl Lagerfeld), who would go on to found a successful fashion label under her own name after moving to London. Living upstairs in the mansardes (small quarters, previously reserved for maids that are located on the top floor right under the roof of apartment buildings in France), was, among others, a French/Egyptian couple, who ran a travel agency and restored old furniture. A young group of jazz musicians also lived for a short while on my floor.

As with most French apartment buildings, we had a guardienne (formerly known as a concierge), who was Portuguese, and would actually save my life years later in 2008 by calling the *pompiers* (firemen) when I suddenly fell in my apartment and couldn't get to a phone. Delivering the mail to the front door of my apartment as she did every day (she didn't have a separate set of keys), she was able to hear me call for help from my hallway, where I had been lying on the floor for a few hours.

As is the case with many old Parisian buildings, the firemen had to enter from the outside through the front of the building, which they did by extending their ladder up to my fourth-level floor and breaking one of the old 10-foot tall double-pane windows that separated the salon from the balcony. Once they found me, I was transported by ambulance to one of the oldest hospitals in the world, the Hôpital Hôtel-Dieu on the Isle de la Cité near Notre Dame Cathedral of Paris, with the emergency team checking my vital signs every few minutes.

Known for its excellent 21st century emergency care, the original building of the Hôtel-Dieu dates back to the 7th century. Initially set-up as a charity that provided food and shelter for the poor, the Hôtel-Dieu ("God's House") expanded into a medical center for the sick in the 17th century. Destroyed by a big fire in 1772, it was then rebuilt and, under Napoleon Bonaparte, became a bona fide hospital for curing illnesses and infirmities. The care I received at this revered institution was impressive. Health care in France (paid through taxes) is generally very good. For example, if, at any time (day or night), you get sick in Paris, you can phone a service called 'SOS Médecins' (SOS Doctors), and for 50 Euros (about $50), the doctor on duty will make a house call within the hour – something unheard of in the United States.

Back in 1995, however, I was the proud, new permanent resident of a lovely old Parisian apartment, eager to engage with my new surroundings. Intent on expanding my knowledge of art, I became a member of the Musée du Louvre and began taking art history courses (History of Art, Impressionism, Egyptian Art, etc.) there. On a more practical side, I also began looking for a contractor and the city's best suppliers of marble tiles to upgrade my rooms – a challenge, but a thoroughly enjoyable project. My daughter, Stephanie, came to Paris to help me with the renovation and designed a large *armoire* (closet), which was added to the front entrance. Wall tile was changed in the kitchen and two bathrooms, a state-of-the-art washing machine, installed in the kitchen, toilets, upgraded, and the master bathtub and sink adjacent to my bedroom, replaced. The entire apartment was repainted, and fabric was added to the walls in my second bedroom. It wasn't perfect, but for the next 16 years – whether I was waking up to daylight filtering through the louvered 10 foot–high shutters of the salon or watching the twinkling Eiffel Tower lights at night – it was a home that I absolutely loved.

During this time, as I stayed in touch with my friends in Germany and around the world, I also made a number of new ones: a young lawyer, married to a banker, who handled my

The garden setting of one of Paris' private clubs, the Cercle de l'Union Interalliée, close to my home. When I was not entertaining friends and family – such as my grandson, Tony – it was where I did my swimming for close to 15 years.

lease, Nicole Ordonneau; a Romanian painter (now deceased) by the name of Joana Celibidache, who was the widow of a well-known Romanian orchestra conductor, Sergiu Celibidache; and a now-retired French-American educator, Patricia Monacelli, who taught English at the Hautes Etudes Commerciales (HEC), Paris' top business school, and was director of an association of American university graduates called PAN (Paris Alumni Network). I also renewed my contact with members of the large Parisian Romanian community, including a group of modern dancers and choreographers, with whom I had toured in France in the 1980s under the Théatre Choréographique de Rennes, Gigi Caciuleanu, Dan Mastacan, and Ruxandra "Ruxie" Racovitze, who taught modern dance at the University of Paris. She and her husband, Philippe Morel, remain among my closest friends. I also reconnected with past foreign service friends like Odette Millot, the wife of the French consul general to Frankfurt when we lived there, who later became the French ambassador to Germany. I am so pleased to be in touch with all of them to this day.

As time passed, I settled into life in Paris and gave up commuting between Paris and Berlin. As an older widow now living alone in Paris (with no expectations of any future romance), I began to create a new world around me. This included joining the Cercle de l'Union Interalliée, a social club originally formed at the onset of World War I for Allied officers and diplomats.

The Louvre Museum and architect I.M. Pei's glass pyramid, two metro
stops from my apartment. One of the largest and most visited museums
in the world, it is where I took art history and sketching classes.

Located on Rue du Faubourg Saint-Honoré in a beautiful old Parisian mansion, it is one of the
more distinguished international private clubs in Paris. I joined it primarily for its lovely pool
and facilities and it took six months for me to be sponsored and accepted. It was there that I
began swimming laps several times a week – a practice I continue to this day. The time and the
effort invested in the club's long application process (with some helpful contacts) were well
worth it, as there was always something to do or attend at the center. Facilities at the Cercle
included lovely reception and dining rooms in the styles of Louis XV and XVI, and an attractive
terrace overlooking a beautiful garden, where I could easily invite people to join me for tea,
drinks or dinner. There were lectures and movies, as well as an extensive library that was always
accessible. No more than a 15-minute walk from my apartment, this club became an important
anchor for me, and one of the highlights of my life in Paris.

I also sought out 2 additional associations: the American Library of Paris and the Paris
Alumni Network (PAN), an organization that connects American, Paris-based college graduates
with one-another (out of more than 150,000 expat Americans living in France today, more than

50,000 live in Paris). The American Library sponsored a variety of programs and outings, and through it, I had the pleasure one evening of meeting the legendary American actor Gregory Peck shortly before his death in 2003. He was then in his 80s and had been married for almost 50 years to his French wife Véronique – a former journalist with the newspaper France Soir – whom he had met on the set of Roman Holiday, his famous 1953 film with Audrey Hepburn. He was one of many well-known actors, writers, and artists to give lectures there.

Keeping an eye on the world of dance and theater, I also entered a more introspective period and began to explore other possible hidden talents of my own, including sketching and painting (the physical beauty of Paris surrounding you at all times just has a way of inspiring you to do so). So along with the art history courses at the Louvre, I tried my hand at several private drawing classes (*classes de dessin*) in charcoal, red chalk (*sanguine*), and colored pencil. The classes were usually held in and around the museum.

Indoors, in one of the Louvre's famous antiquity halls filled with exquisitely chiseled sculptures, we would draw careful replicas of Egyptian, Greek or Roman marble statues under the critical eye of our professor, and learn about concepts of shadow and light. Outside, in the nearby Jardin des Tuileries (Tuileries Gardens), we would morph into impressionists for an entire morning, and attempt to record the soft spirit of flowers and trees as families strolled by with their children. I very much looked forward to these outings, and my artwork, though never great, improved over time.

Physically, I had, of course, given up ballet classes long ago, though I did continue to do stretching excercises, and spent a lot of time walking through the city to different destinations, especially to outdoor markets and specialty stores to shop for food. My marketplace of choice was at the Place de la Madeleine, where I would buy the freshest French patés, cheeses, fruits, and vegetables. On my way home, I would stop at Fouquet's, famous for its *patisseries* (pastries) and exotic fruits, then a *boulangerie* (bread shop) for the crustiest baguettes. At times, I would also buy some caviar at a store simply called "Caviar" that specialized in dozens of types of fish roe and caviar, and end up at a local *charcuterie* (butcher shop) in my neighborhood. I would pile everything into one of those typical French rollerbags used for groceries and wheel it back to my apartment.

For the more immediate staples, the Monoprix department store up the Champs-

Paris as seen through master painters of the 20th century, and some of the paintings that inspired me to take classes at the Louvre: (clockwise) *Pont St. Michel*, by Henri Matisse; *Street in Montmartre*, by Maurice Utrillo; *La Place de l'Opéra*, by Ulpiano Checa y Sanz; *Luxembourg Gardens, Monument to Chopin*, by Henri Rousseau; and *The Bride of Notre Dame*, by Marc Chagall.

Elysees would do. I would walk up this famous avenue, past crowds of people, young and old, representing hundreds of nationalities (including women from the Emirates in black burkas) – to the Monoprix, down a flight of stairs and into its very congested lower floor where groceries and other household items were sold. The building had no elevators and whatever you bought had to be carried up by hand. This was perhaps one of the trade-offs to living in Paris. The city has never been known for the comfort and ease of living that are usually associated with daily life in the United States. Nevertheless, I loved interacting – for good or bad – with the Parisians themselves and hearing the French language (something I miss very much these days in the United States). I was assiduous about reading both the French papers of Le Monde and Le Figaro as well as the International Herald Tribune (now the International New York Times) every day. My television was almost always tuned to the French *chaines* (channels) for the old French movies with Yves Montand, Simone Signoret, Jean Paul Belmondo, Jean Gabin, Jeanne Moreau, Catherine Deneuve, etc. or to CNN or France Inter for the latest news.

With ballet, dance, opera, and theater never too far from my heart, I, like so many other Parisians, also became part of the theater-going public. After years of organizing theater and dance performances for others, it was now my turn to finally cross over to the audience full-time – without any responsibility other than to find my seat and enjoy the show. Of course, there was always much to see in Paris: a new art exhibit at the Musée d'Orsay, the Grand Palais, or the Musée Picasso; a *vernissage* (exhibit opening) honoring an artist at a local gallery nearby, an invitation to a fashion show at Dior or Lanvin. There was an embarrassment of riches between those events and the very enticing selection of theater, dance, or concerts offered by the city. One of my favorite theatrical events became attending the performances of the magnificent Palais Garnier Opera House, and no season went by without catching the rising stars of the Paris Opera Ballet. The legendary Théâtre des Champs-Elysées on Avenue Montaigne was equally important to me, as it presented unusual productions that kept me connected to contemporary trends, and since this theater was so close to my home (literally in the park across the street), I often subscribed to a full season of tickets. I also made a point of regularly attending the latest French productions of the classical Comédie Française.

The years in Paris went by quickly. The city offered a plethora of exciting choices for me – whether it was an invitation for lunch at the Hotel Plaza Athenée, attending the famous

Horse-drawn carriages and stagecoaches in front of
the Paris Opera, Palais Garnier, around 1896

Longchamps horse races, or just sitting down for an expresso at a local café after a long walk
through the city – a wonderful pastime in itself, where I could stare at pedestrians and fashions,
police on horseback, or the latest brands of French and European cars that never stopped
honking. On my way home, I then could stop at the Galeries Lafayette, Paris' largest department
store, and ride (by modern elevator no less!) to its top floor for the most amazing array of food
delicacies; or window-shop on the elegant Faubourg St. Honoré and Avenue Montaigne past
boutiques filled with beautiful designer cashmere sweaters and handbags. And, after watching
the changing of the guards at the Elysée Palace close to my apartment, I could happily return
home to my comfortable abode, proud of my efforts for that day.

My children visited several times a year, and when my grandson Tony was six years
old, he came to Paris for the first time while my daughter, Stephanie, was on a photographic

Inside the majestic Palais Garnier Opera (left), home to the largest stage in Europe. It was the setting for the novel, *Phantom of the Opera*, and subsequent Lloyd-Webber musical. Its famous ceiling (right), re-painted in 1964 by Marc Chagall on a mobile frame, features opera scenes by 14 composers, including Verdi, Bizet, Mozart, and Wagner.

assignment for National Geographic. We spent time in the Tuileries Gardens, took a trip down the Seine on a Bateau Mouche, which he remembers as one of the best moments of his trip, and took a few art classes for children at the Centre Pompidou, where he showed a talent for drawing. A few years later, and a bit older, he stayed with me again in Paris. He was about 12 years old, and I decided to take him on a stroll through the famous area of Montmartre – with its Moulin Rouge and Place Pigalle nightlife. We watched as artists painted scenes around the Sacré Coeur Basilica, hoping to sell a painting or two to one of thousands of tourists eager for a souvenir of the 130 foot-tall hill that at one time or another had been the home to many famous painters, including Pablo Picasso, Salvador Dali, and Henri Toulouse-Lautrec. We spent time in the Musée d'Orsay, the museum known for its wonderful Impressionist collections of Cézannes, Van Goghs, Monets, and Renoirs (among many others), and though he was a bit disappointed at learning that trains no longer ran at what had once been a train station (the Gare d'Orsay), he thoroughly enjoyed the paintings – as well as a subsequent visit to Disneyland on the outskirts of Paris. As a family, we would later tour the Loire Valley, with its wonderful *chateaux* (castles) – and would treasure that memory for a long time.

A symbol of elegance and beauty, Notre Dame Cathedral, on Isle de la Cité, glows at dusk

When it became clear that I would live with greater ease and comfort in the United States, and be closer to my daughters, I closed this long European chapter of my life with great regret, and, in 2009, uprooted myself one last time for a permanent move back to the United States, where I settled in Sarasota, Florida.

The City of Lights, however, will forever be etched in my mind.

A testament to the resilience of Paris, the Arc de Triomple is lit up with red, white and blue colors of the French flag for the 2016 New Year

10. Sarasota

aris became my home for 18 years, and I loved every minute of it; but after living overseas for almost 60 years, and with the onset of several health issues, I began to think about returning to the United States for good.

We had lived abroad since 1948, and while our family had witnessed history unfolding around the globe, we had also missed – for better or for worse – a myriad of important events at home: the devastating effects of McCarthyism; the Korean War; the civil rights marches against racial segregation; Martin Luther King's *"I Have a Dream"* speech in Washington, DC; the enactment of the Voting Rights Act; the integration of our schools; the creation of NASA and the excitement in the U.S. over Neil Armstrong's landing on the moon; the assassinations of President John F. Kennedy, Robert F. Kennedy, and Martin Luther King; the Cuban Missile Crisis and Invasion of the Bay of Pigs; the hippie movement of the 1960s and Woodstock; the launch of rock and roll with Chuck Berry, Jerry Lee Lewis, and Elvis Presley; the arrival of the Beatles in the U.S.; the protests against the Vietnam War; President Lyndon B. Johnson's Great Society reforms and the final passing of Medicare and Medicaid; the riots of Watts, Detroit, and New York City; the fight for women's rights and the Equal Rights Amendment; the conflict over Roe

Thunderstorm clouds gather over a waterfront pier and playground
in Sarasota on a typical summer evening

v. Wade; the untangling of the Watergate scandal and President Richard M. Nixon's resignation; the elation over the success of the First Gulf War; the frenzy over Apple's inauguration of the Mac desktop, the computer revolution, and the Internet – to name but a few of them.

We, of course, kept up with these significant events through newspapers, television, and visits home to family, but we were physically removed from their epicenter, and could only appreciate them from afar.

As I contemplated my options in coming back to the United States, I learned from a friend of mine, MaryLynn Fixler, about a small city situated on the Gulf Coast of Florida, south of Tampa, called Sarasota. MaryLynn was concert manager of the Sarasota Orchestra at the time. She suggested I visit Sarasota in the winter because of its warm and welcoming climate. I followed her advice, loved the city, and began renting an apartment there during the winter months for the next several years, becoming a "snowbird" as I shuttled back and forth from Paris.

With both of my daughters now living in the United States, and my health becoming more fragile (I had taken several falls in Paris), I eventually decided to give up the commute and, in 2007, purchased a lovely apartment in the center of the city overlooking much of downtown

Now in my nineties, sitting at home close to my
most cherished family photos and memories

Sarasota and the Gulf of Mexico. And that is where I am now, recalling the wonderful memories of my past 90 plus years.

After putting up with several operations and rehabilitations (the usual hip and knee replacements that come with aging), my daughter, Stephanie, decided to move from Maryland to Florida to be close by. I also engaged the help of a lovely person from Bogotá, Colombia, Martha Cerquera, a married mother of two successful sons (an engineer and a doctor) for my daily chores. She has been invaluable to me for the past seven years, helping me several hours a day during the week with shopping, cleaning, cooking, and the like.

Aging, as we know, is no fun, but thankfully, I can still live independently. After a vibrant and fulfilling life, punctuated by continuous activity around the globe, it was, at first difficult for me to adjust to a slower, more sedentary pace. More importantly, it was a challenge to accept the gradual deterioration of my faculties, limited mobility, hearing loss, and at times, just plain boredom. But I managed to adapt – and I hope, gracefully…. The Pulitzer prize-winning author and critic, Leon Edel, once said, "The answer to old age is to keep one's mind busy and go on with one's life as if it were interminable." So that is what I have chosen to do….

While I spend much of my time reading, watching old Turner classic movies on TV, and reminiscing about my life, loves, and world travels, my daughter Stephanie sees to it that all my medical and social needs are met. And my other daughter, Lauri, now living in South Carolina with her own family – her husband, Warren Davis, and son, Donte – visits me regularly once a month. Both have been a great comfort and convinced me that, in addition to keeping one's mind occupied and one's health in check through mindfulness and exercise, it is essential to have the support of a good social network – whether it's family, friends or both. And if you can combine these assets with positive thinking and expressions of gratitude, they can help guide you toward a long, healthy life.

Saying farewell to Paris was painful and stressful. Not only was I leaving the city of my dreams behind for good, I was also bidding farewell to my beloved Europe – with all of its cultural karma that had become part of my soul. And who knew what lay ahead?

My daughter, Stephanie, had overseen a very exhausting move from Paris to Sarasota in 2009, and spent weeks in the bowels of my Paris apartment, sorting through two smelly cellars bursting at the seams with more than 100 cartons and pieces of furniture from around the world. Sealed for decades under layers of dust, and many still in their original wrappings, hundreds of objects and mementos came to light, a testimony to a life well lived and traveled. These cartons – and the memories associated with them – were what remained of all of our globe-trotting adventures and my work, and I had a difficult time leaving them behind. Each carton or wrapping revealed a particular secret, a connection to the past: Indian copper lamps, Italian pottery, German glass, French coffee tables, Pakistani rugs, Japanese kimonos, Korean chests, Moroccan wall hangings, Filipino peacock chairs, Greek worry beads, Chinese wood carvings – and loads of books in dozens of languages, family albums with photographs from every corner of the earth, vinyl records and tapes, and of course, hundreds of programs and posters of my productions…. While many items returned with me to the United States, those that were deemed unimportant were simply discarded along with the rest of the trash – a process that was agonizing for me at times. After all, this was a final parting with the past, with memories sealed and briefly resurrected, some of which hadn't been accessed for over 50 years.

After bringing the contents down to a workable load, we prepared for shipping and were amazed to see how the moving companies in France actually remove the contents from the old Paris apartments: An automated pulley mechanism is installed on the outside of the building, and all the furniture and cartons are lowered on movable planks from the windows or balconies down to the vans waiting below – a practice that, except for the electrical controls, probably goes back to the Middle Ages.

Once the move was completed, I settled into Sarasota and began to take advantage of the many quality cultural attractions offered by the city: the Sarasota Ballet, the Asolo Repertory Theater, the Sarasota Opera, the Ringling Museum, the Sarasota Film Festival, etc. I also enrolled in several writing classes, and, in the process, made new friendships.

This small, charming city with a current population of no more than 55,000 year-round residents (swelling to more than twice its size in the warm winter months with the arrival of northern snowbirds and students eager to take advantage of beach life during their semester breaks), is perfect for a retired or semi-retired person or for those seeking a slower pace and more serenity in their daily lives. The natural beauty of its beaches and wildlife on keys such as Siesta, Lido, Ana Marie Island, and Longboat makes this 'Sunshine Coast' a haven for sports and wildlife enthusiasts, cultural aficionados, and families with children – though much of its population is over the age of 65. Having lived all

Our moving company in action: Furniture and cartons were loaded onto an electric ladder outside the building, with a liftgate that extended up to our windows and balcony, and then lowered the contents to the ground.

Peace and tranquility permeate the natural beauty of the
Sarasota region, with clear blue beach waters, a lush bird
sanctuary on Lido Key nearby, and the occasional appearance
of one of the Gulf's most famous visitors, the blue heron

Known for its cool, white sands, Siesta Beach – one of America's finest – paints an alluring picture in turquoise and white as it welcomes "snowbirds" and seagulls to its pristine shores, along with many tourists eager for some fun and relaxation

Among Sarasota's many cultural draws, Seward Johnson's "Unconditional Surrender" statue locally known as the "Kissing Statue", at the city's Marina

my life in large, hyperactive cities that offered a variety of cultural activities simultaneously, it took a while for me to get used to the quieter and gentler pace of this southern city, but it was a welcomed change.

With time – and confronted with added physical limitations that resulted from my recent operations (needing a walker for the first time, for example) – I came to realize how beneficial this new lifestyle could be to one's health and soul, so that I have now embraced it completely. There is nothing like the process of aging to remind you of your gradual physical (and at times mental) decline, and having somewhat less stimulation around you may be a blessing. So as a result, after galavanting around the world for decades, in a life filled with rich and exciting experiences, I have "settled down," become a bit more sedentary, and probably more philosophical and accepting about what invariably lies ahead. These days, I have also come to realize that being more of a homebody is not such a bad thing after all.

Be that as it may, embarking on a more peaceful and quieter phase of my life has not meant that I have become disinterested in the world at large. Quite the contrary: My interest in the cultural scene has never been stronger and I, with my daughters often as my dates, will find something interesting to do, whether it's watching a must-see film, catching the latest theatrical performance at the Asolo (a wonderful rep company), attending an evening of the now well-known Sarasota Ballet, checking out the Marina's "Unconditional Surrender" statue (based on photographs by Alfred Eisenstaedt and Victor Jorgenson), or just going out for a dinner of sushi and tempura as a family to our favorite Japanese restaurant. For the more adventurous days, there are always those sun-drenched crystal white beaches and aquamarine waters of the Gulf, beckoning you to watch the glorious parade of wildlife go by.

Then, sometimes, I find myself falling back on my old habit of looking for talent – a potential production to offer to a theater in the U.S. or in Europe, especially if it's top quality and different. For example, I saw a very clever and entertaining production at the Asolo Theater several years ago of the "Three Baritones," and my initial reaction was to see if I could take it on tour – perhaps even to Germany. That drive to entertain and inspire audiences – which now remains mostly buried – occasionally rears its head, and I wonder, "What if…?" I begin to reason with myself: "I may be limited physically, but perhaps with the help of a computer and cell phone, I could do it one more time, maybe an international folk dance festival here in Sarasota, or a summer theater festival in Miami. I think it's time for a new project.… " Old habits die slowly or, sometimes, not at all.

Then reality kicks in, and again, I become aware of my frailties.

But it never hurts to dream.

So I return to what has become my passion these past few years and something I can do: swim. I had begun to swim laps years ago at my club in Paris. There is a lovely pool in my building, where I swim several times a week. My goal each time is to reach 20 laps doing the backstroke. As I swim, I look up at the palm trees that shade the pool, and vignettes of my past begin to drift through my mind: the joy I felt skiing down the beautiful mountains of the Alps in Europe, when my body was younger and healthier – Kitzbühel, Cortina d'Ampezzo, Gstaad. I used to be an avid skier (even up to the age of 72), always returning to the slopes despite a number of injuries. It was my husband, Oscar, who had introduced me to skiing, as he did with horseback riding and tennis. I had never skied as a child or an adolescent, and my desire to learn this sport started on our honeymoon in Lake Placid, NY. I remember the wooden skis and the borrowed outfit, and after a few lessons, the freedom of flying down the slopes. Oscar would ski with me for many years, but after an accident, decided that tennis was his sport of choice. I passed on my love of skiing on to my children, who became good at the sport as well.

As I swam my laps one day, the mood in the air was such that it brought me back to my days in India and to a period that had been so pivotal in my life, though I didn't realize it then. I had met so many wonderful people during those three years in New Delhi at the Cecil Hotel: The exotic nature of the place, the exciting and lively gatherings of foreign and local dignitaries, the families from all corners of the world with their children, waiting for their permanent homes to be ready, my good friend Kushwant Singh, who encouraged me with a career in radio. I am reminded of an amusing incident when he took me to visit a temple one day. In India, you must remove your shoes before entering a temple. So Khushwant and I decided to leave our shoes in the car and walk barefoot across the road to the temple, unaware that we had also left our keys in the car, which was locked. I remember how we laughed at our mishap, and how odd we must have looked standing, barefoot, on the side of the road for an hour, trying to flag down another driver, who eventually came to our rescue.

It was also in New Delhi that my career as an impresario began with the wonderful trio of ballet stars, Marina Svetlova, Anton Dolin, and John Gilpin ….

Other images cross my mind: dancing on stage in London; the 80 thunderous curtain calls with Alvin Ailey in Hamburg; exchanging wonderful laughs with Ward Swingle; arguing with my assistant, Manfred….

I think of my past loves, especially Oscar and our adventures together, and the joy I felt when he offered me his very charming marriage proposal. "May I have the permanent priority of your affections and seal it with our engagement?" he had asked so elegantly. I also recall a few other infatuations and the craziness of those times…. Then I wonder whether, after Oscar's death, I should have made more of an effort to contact with my early Romanian friends and first love, Titel, when I heard he had moved to Israel.

I also see my children when they were small: my daughter, Stephanie, directing a gaggle of kids her age from the head of a table at her fourth birthday party in New Delhi, and later, as a teenager, dancing the calypso with Oscar in Ocho Rios, Jamaica, and winning first place in a hotel competition; my daughter, Lauri, ever protective, even at the age of three, talking to flies in my car, urging them to go away and not bother me while I was driving down a street in Frankfurt. Sudden flashes, sudden moments…. How my daughters have grown into good-hearted, creative, and devoted human beings! How proud I am of their achievements, and how grateful I am of my close family and friends!

It's amazing what you can think about when you're swimming on your back – especially at a snail's pace! Or what you can sense… like the rhythmic change of tropical weather filled with gulf breezes, summer heat, and intermittent showers, or the gentle movement of clouds dancing a solitary pas-de-deux against a deep hue of blue beckoning you into an unknown future.

Precious memories are what remain as we age, and soon, they too may just become hazy in the flow of time. Memories that have made me realize how lucky I am to have lived the life I've led, and how privileged I was to have met so many fascinating people! And to think that it all started with ballet and ended with ballet! A classic ballet tour through India as Act I. A contemporary dance company in France as the finale…

I was born with ballet in my soul…. It was the prime motivator that allowed me to pursue my dreams and present programs I treasured to the general public – and it even allowed me to be appreciated for doing so! If I could, I would, in a heartbeat, do it all over again!

It's been a terrific ride, and now, again, it's time to move on…

Feeling a great sense of accomplishment as I complete my
20 swimming laps in our pool – and blow a kiss to all

198

And in the end, it's not the years in your life that count, it's the life in your years.

— Abraham Lincoln

Photo Credits